The
Fantasy
Coloring Book

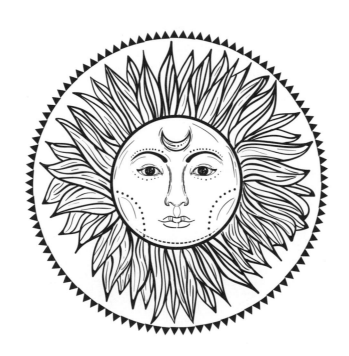

The Fantasy Coloring Book

Enjoy a magical wonder world

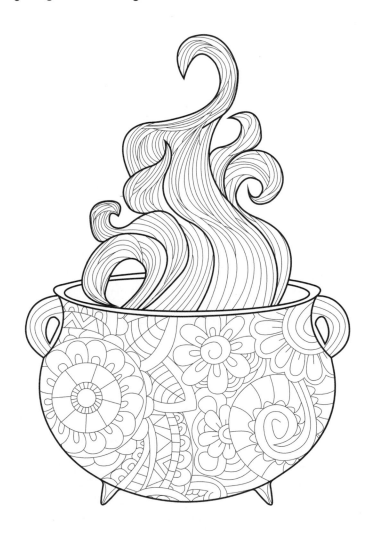

SIRIUS

This edition published in 2023 by Sirius Publishing, a division of
Arcturus Publishing Limited,
26/27 Bickels Yard, 151–153 Bermondsey Street,
London SE1 3HA

ISBN: 978-1-3988-3005-9
CH011155NT

Printed in China

Introduction

Dragons, mermaids, centaurs, wizards—these magnificent creatures live in the imaginative worlds of our storybooks. Fantasy has the power to enchant and bewitch, giving us an escape from reality into a magical realm.

Inside these pages you'll find a collection of mythical creatures, whimsical wildernesses, glorious castles, and artwork fit for a fairy tale. Some pieces are intricate, with detailed patterns and designs, and others are simple in style, leaving the artist with a world of possibilities. No matter if you're a sorcerer or just a fan of being spell bound, there's plenty here to catch your eye. So, whenever you're ready to be transported, find an image that charms you, settle in for a magical ride, and color in the pages of your own story. Your fantasy adventure awaits.

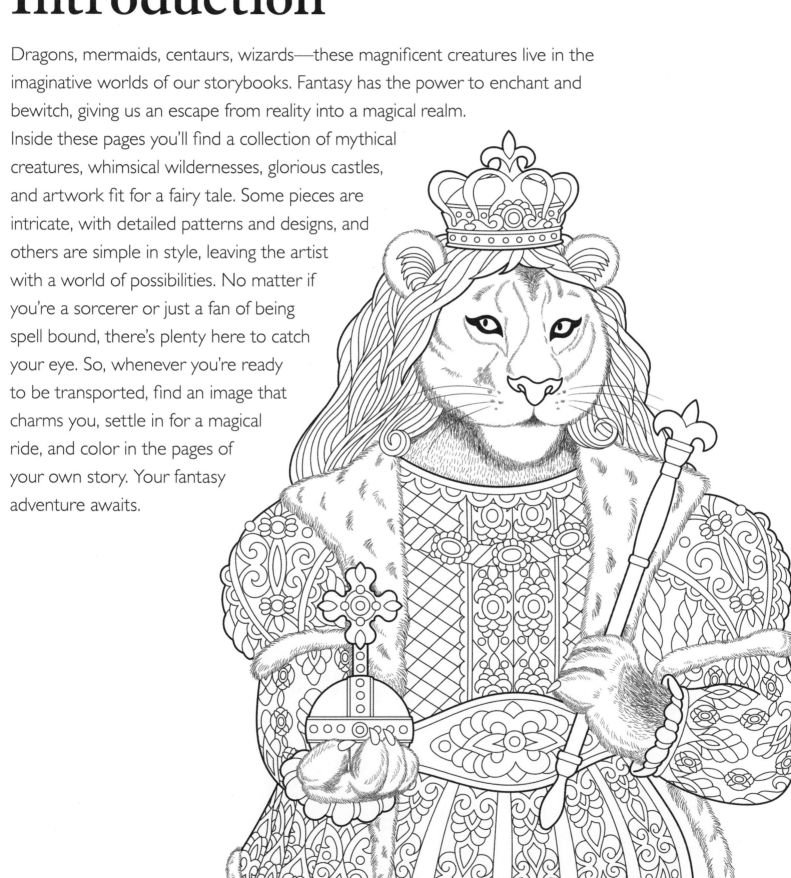

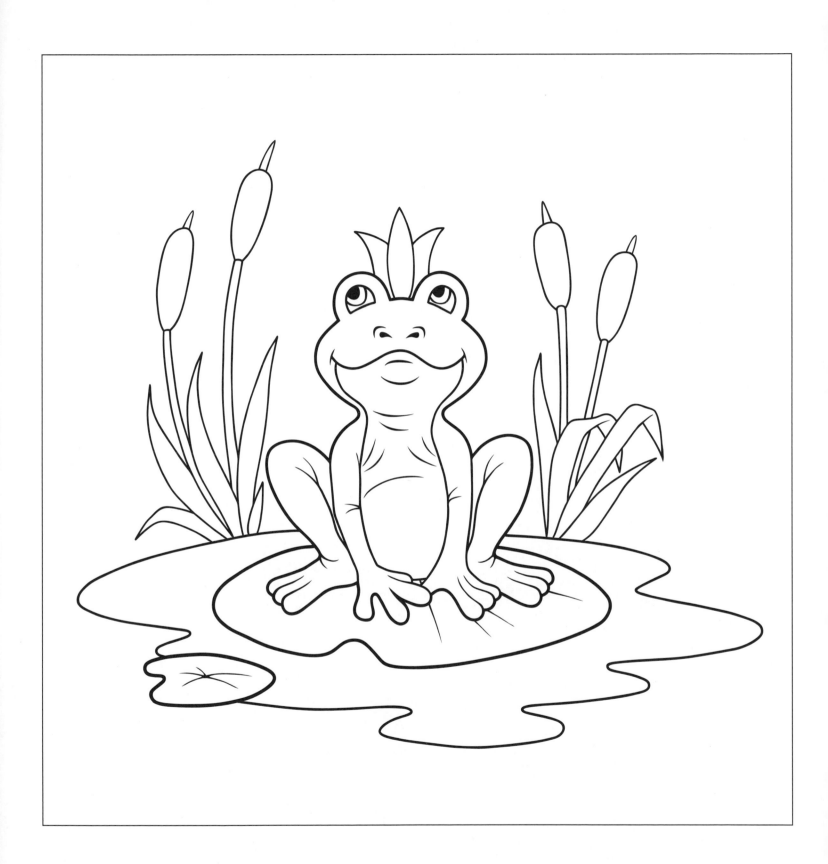

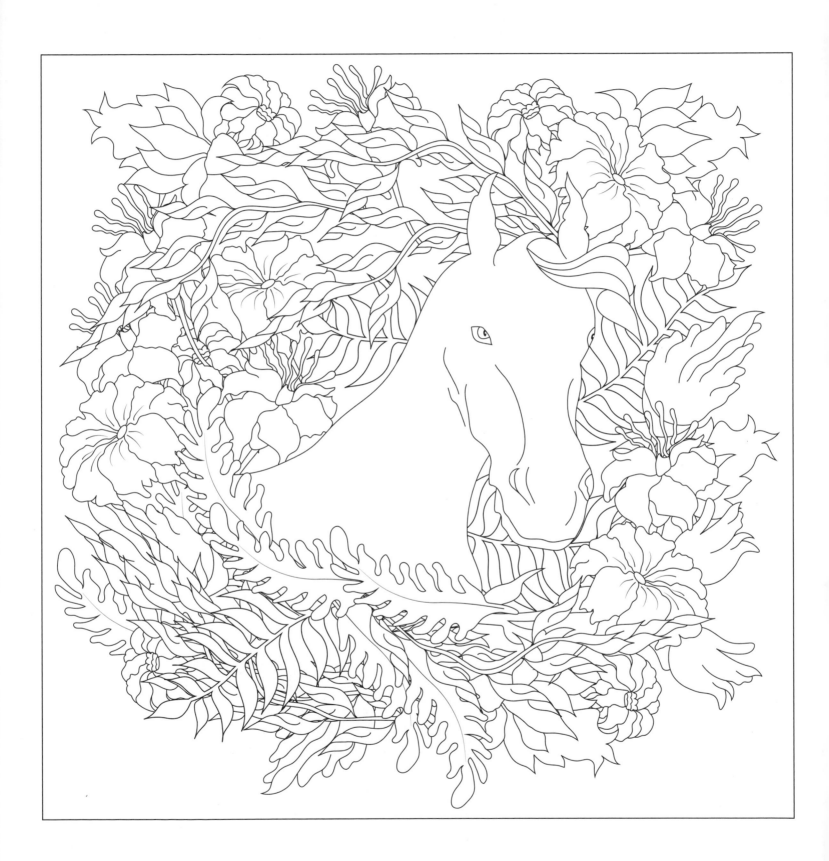

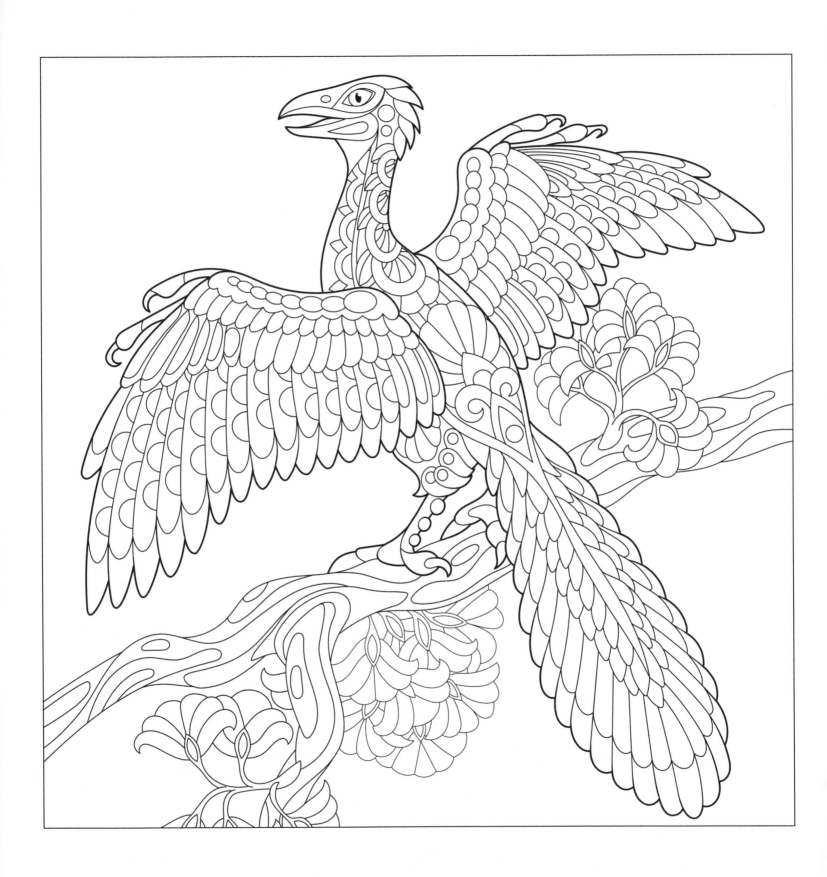

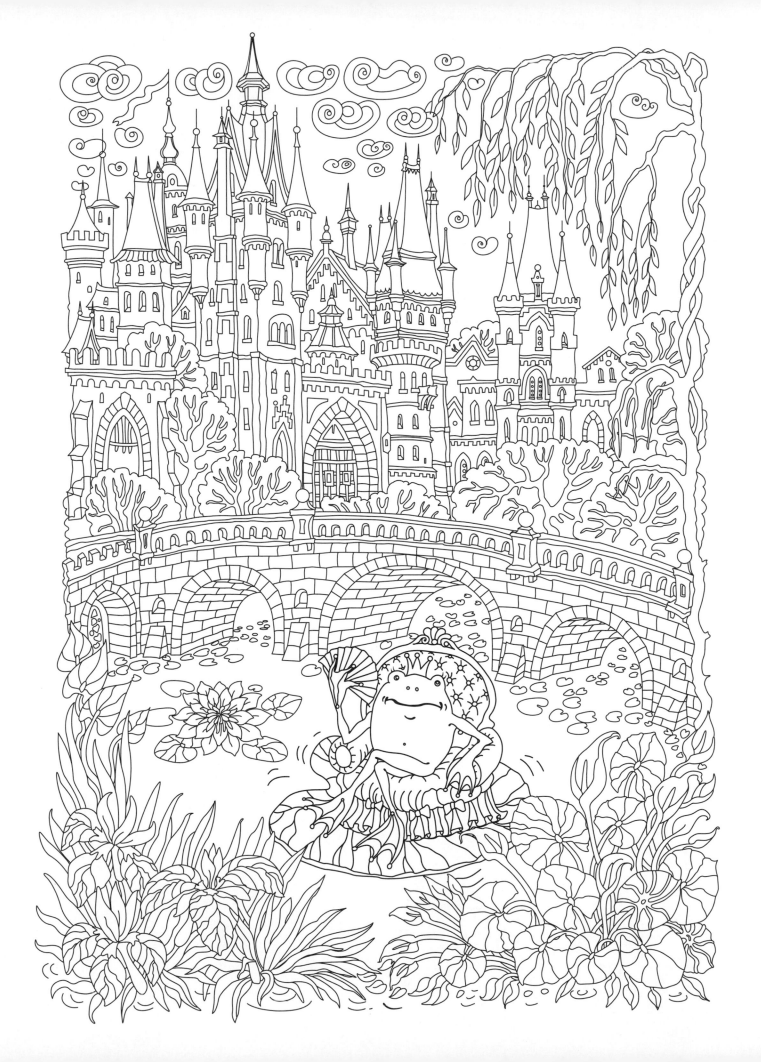

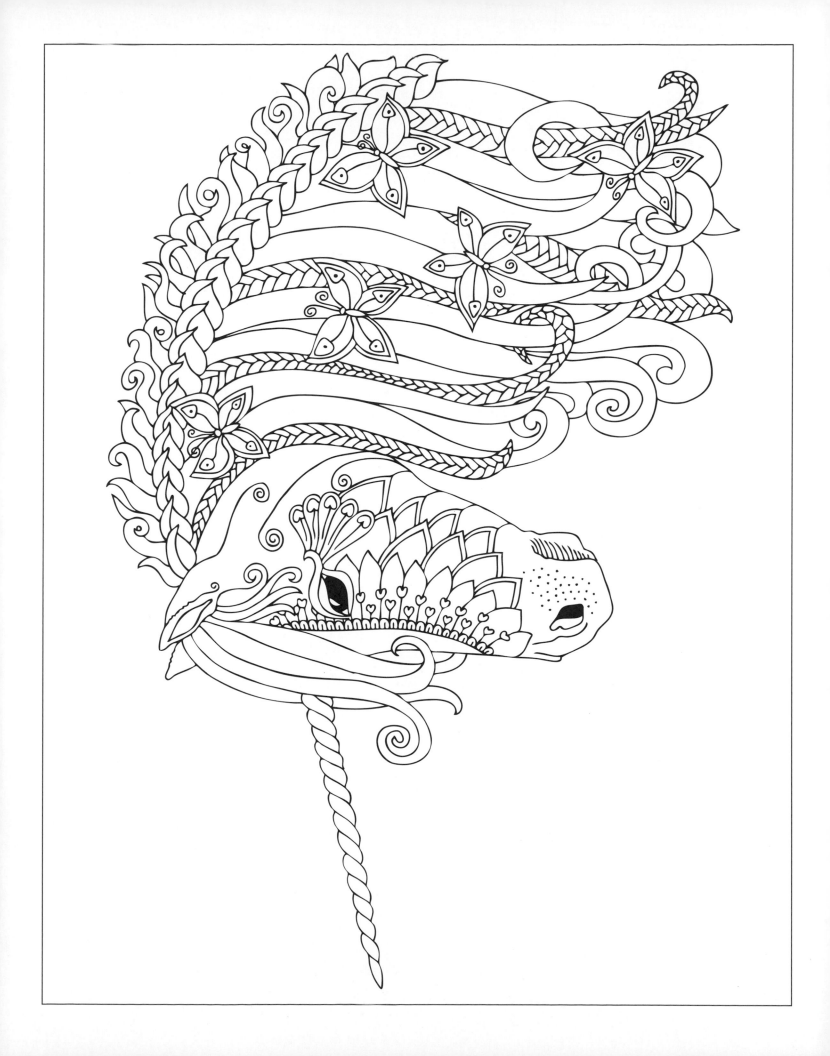

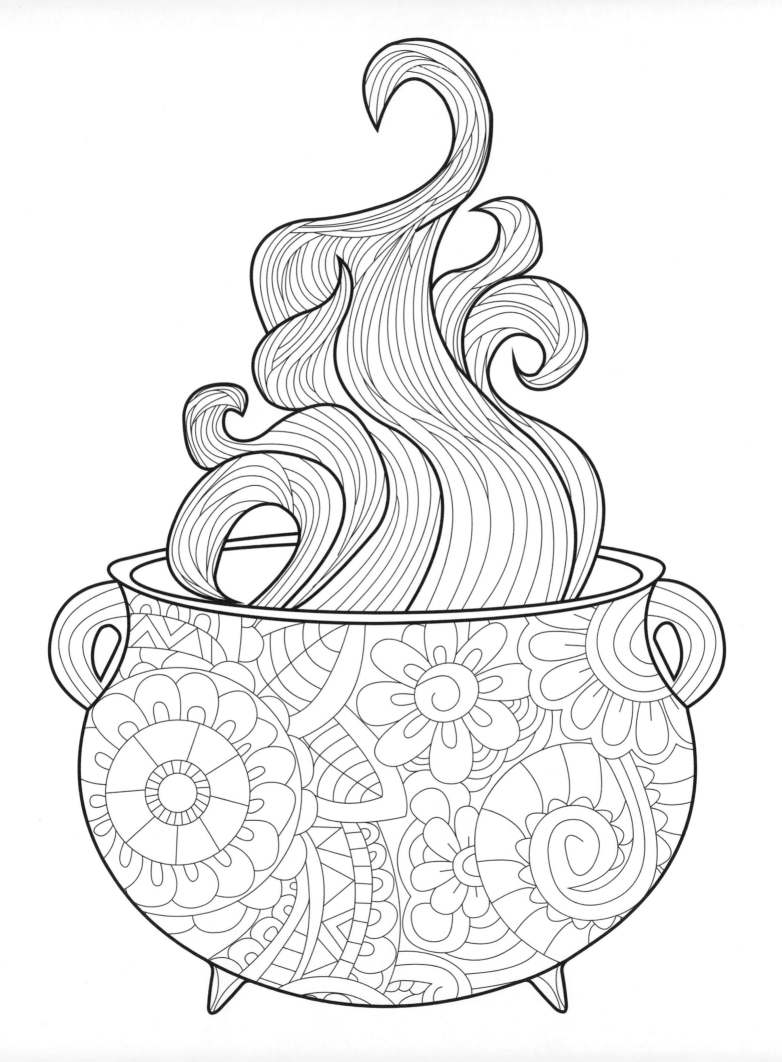

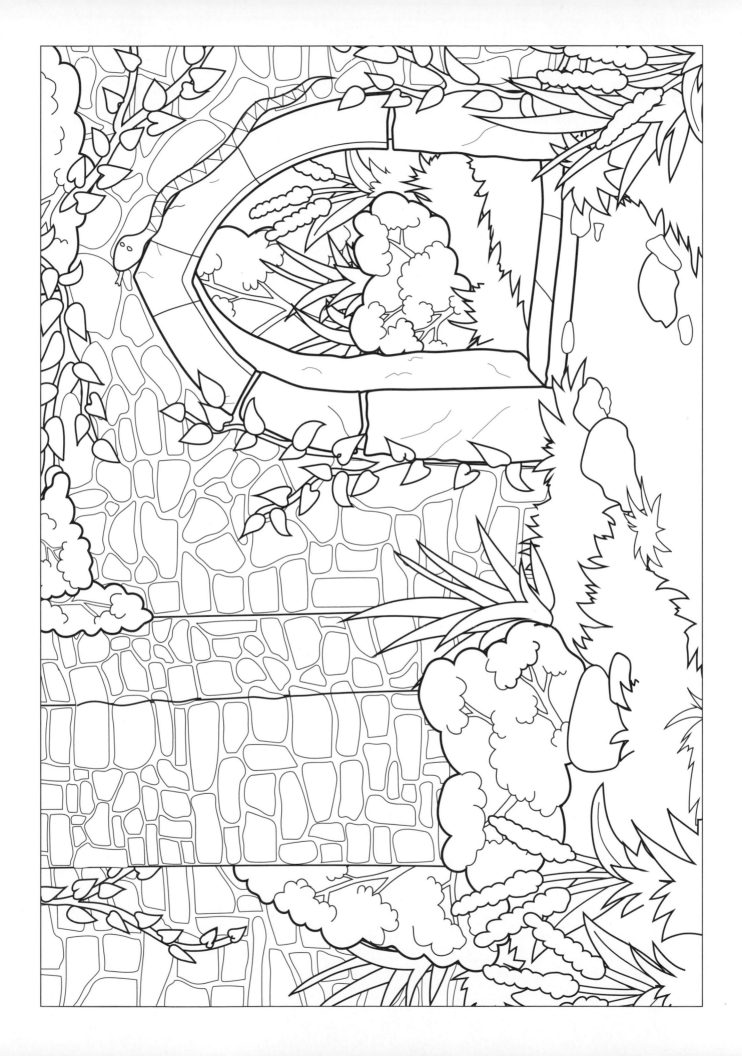

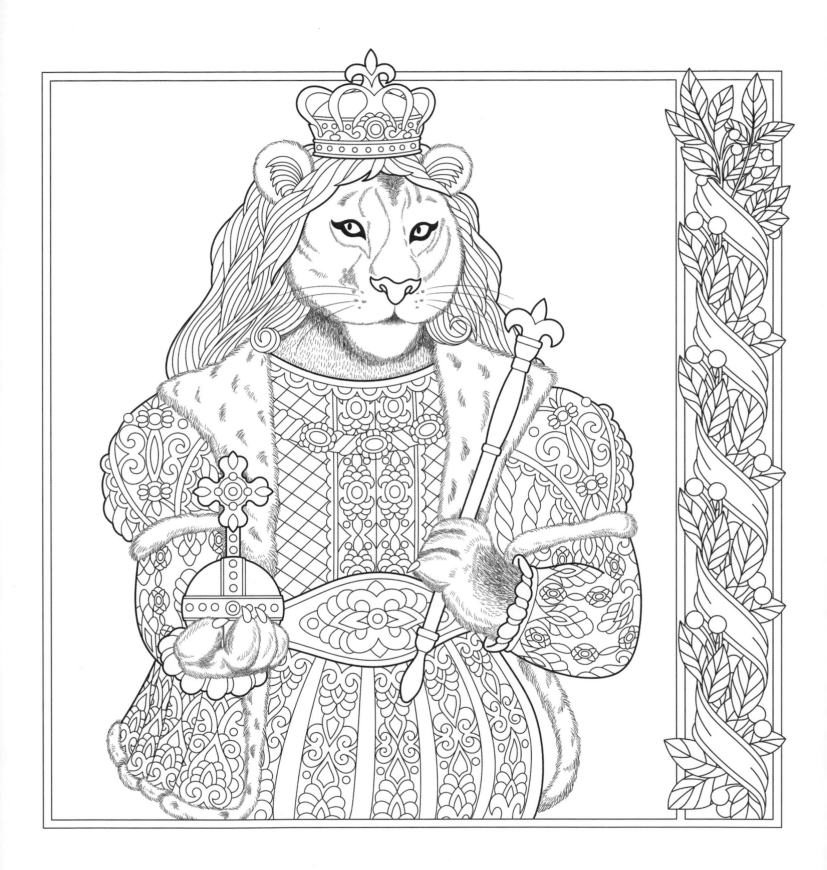

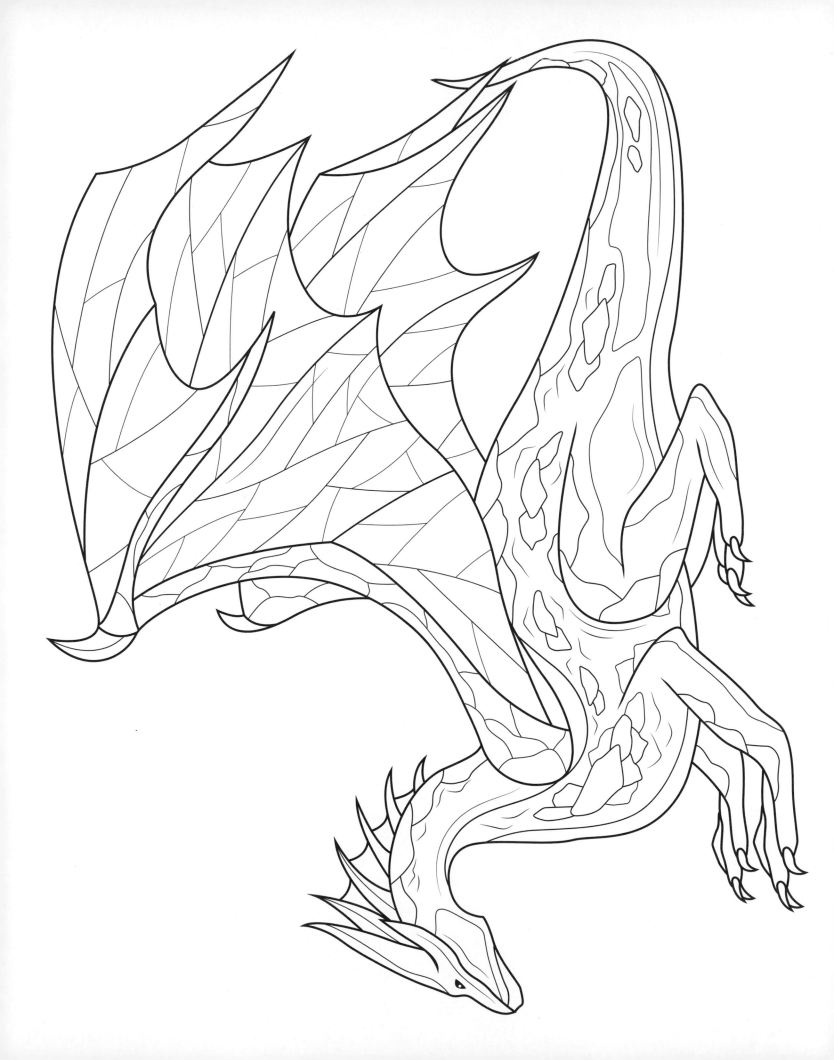

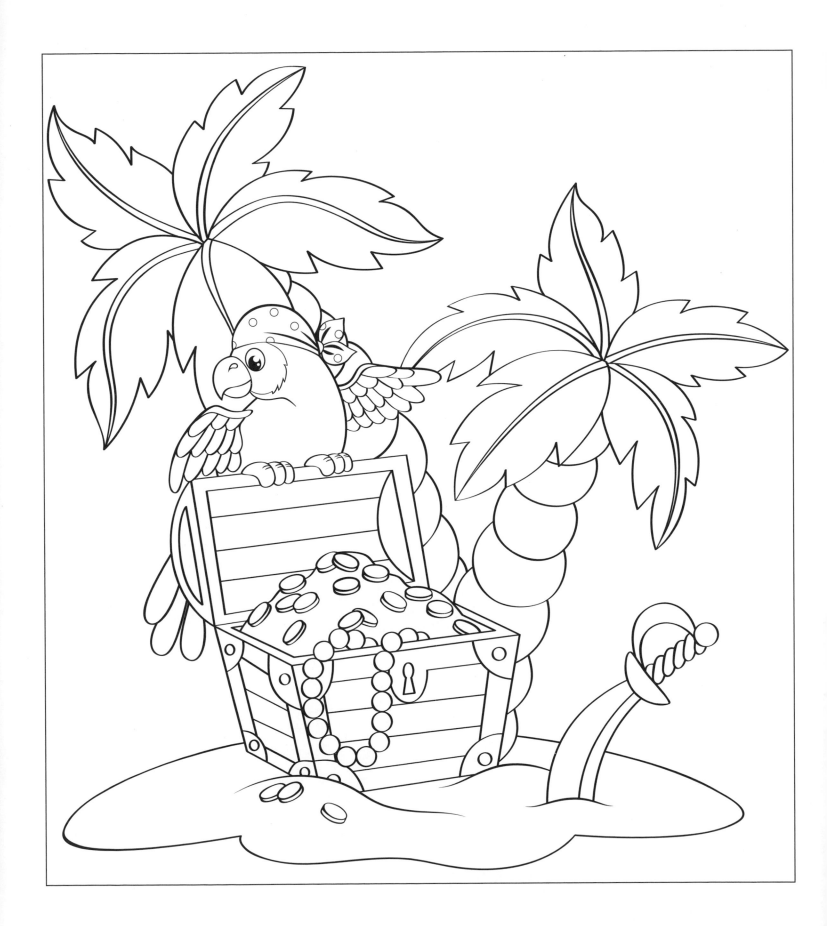

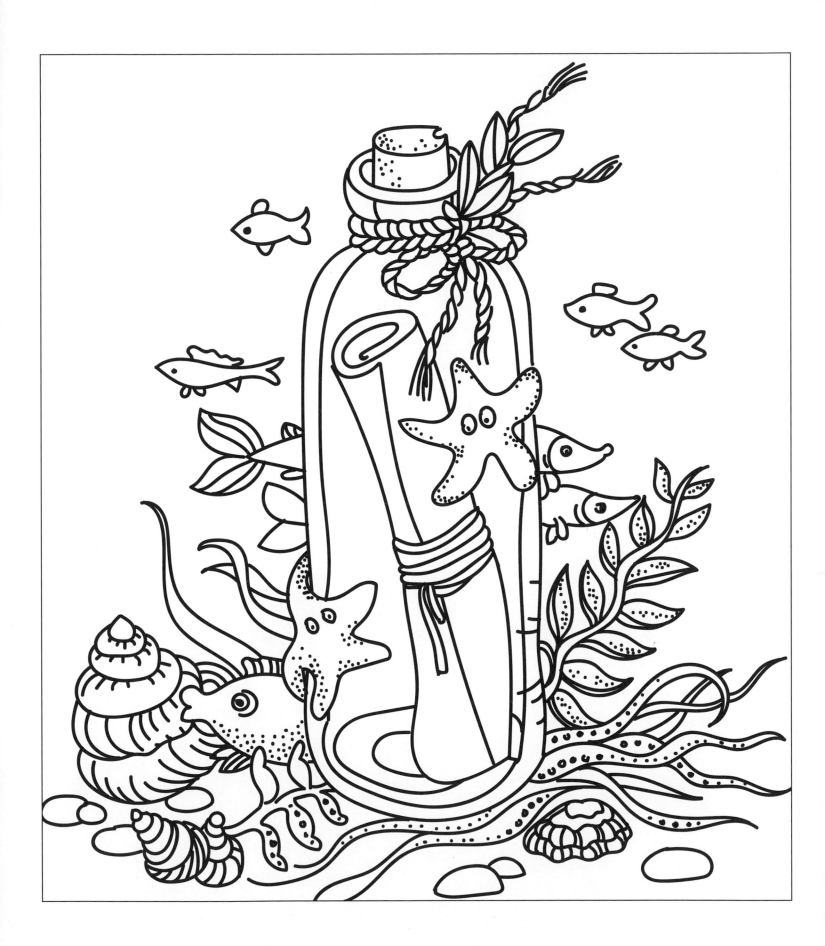

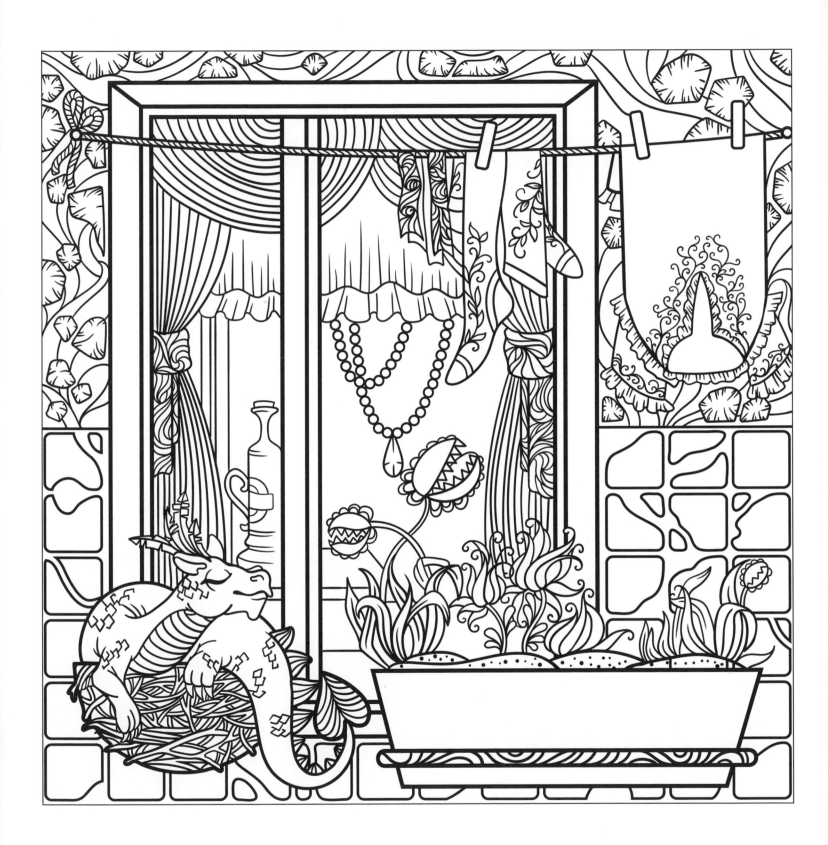

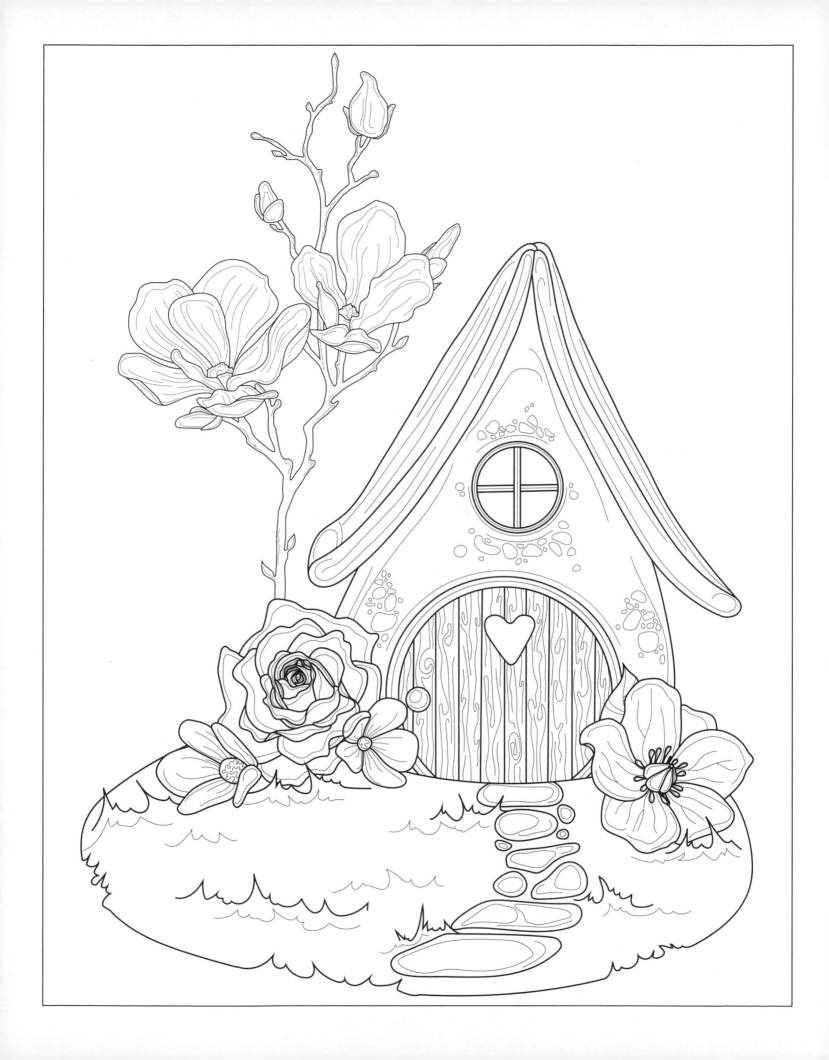

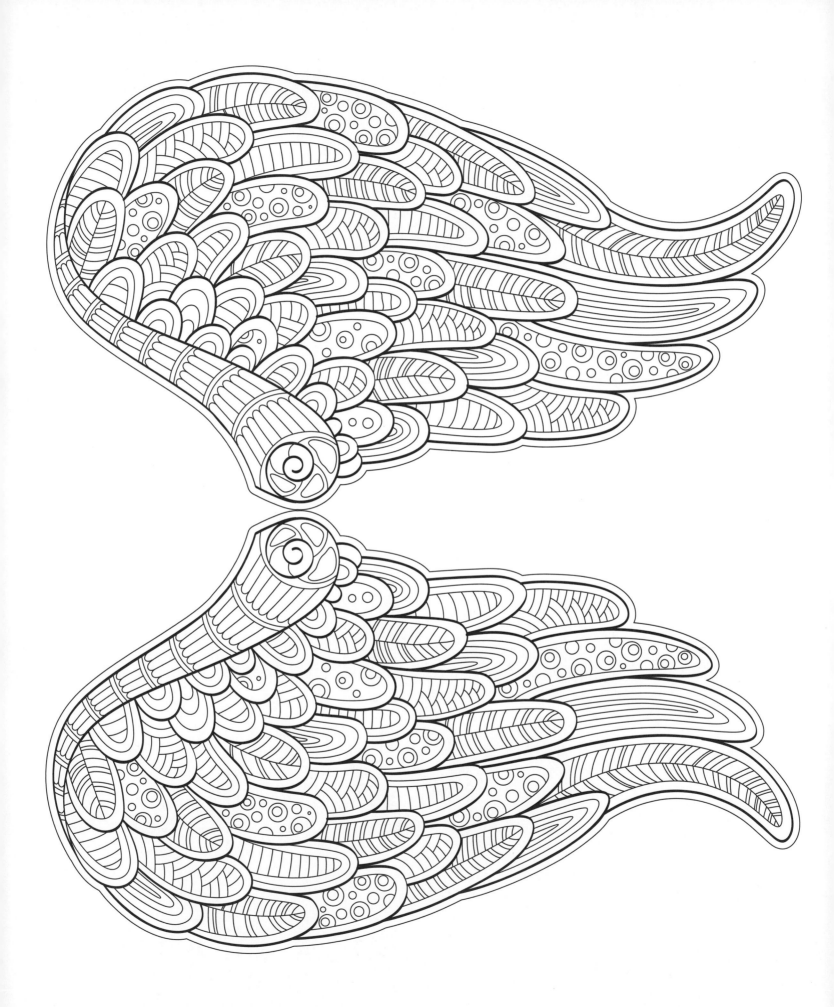

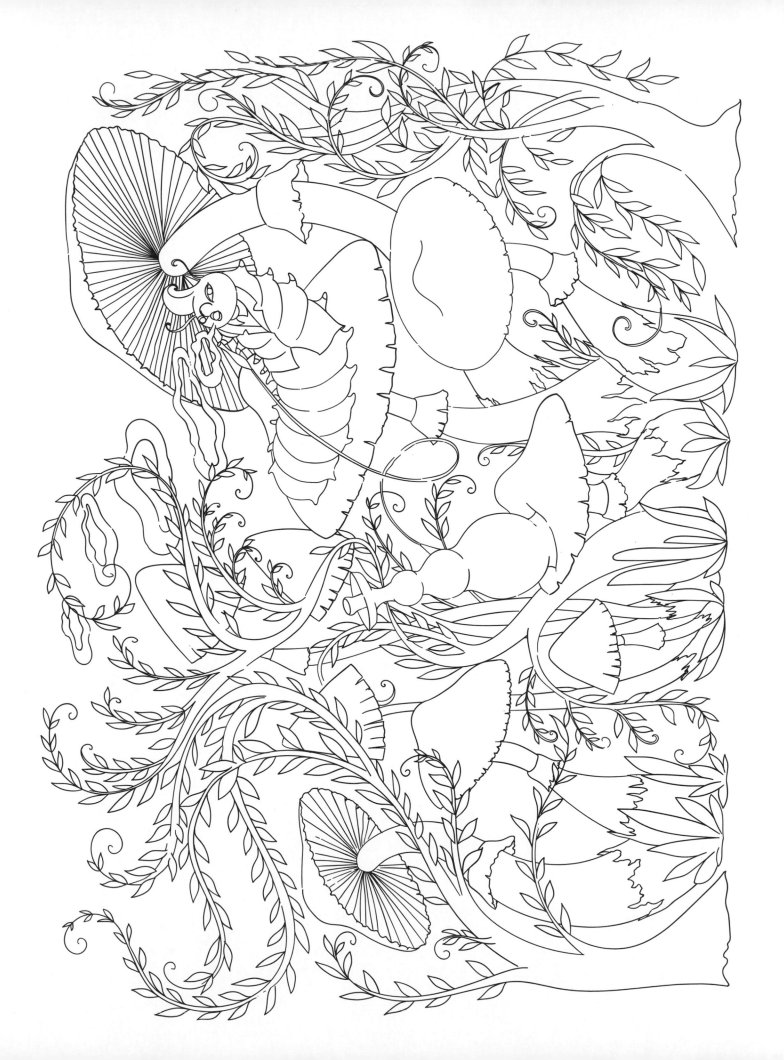

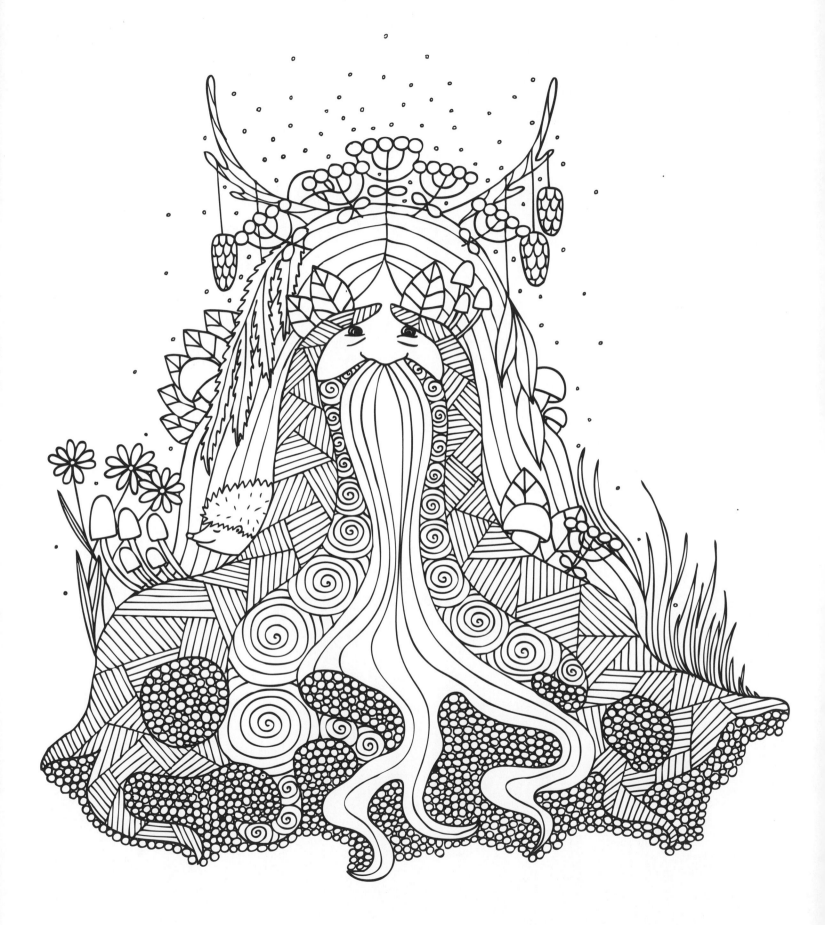

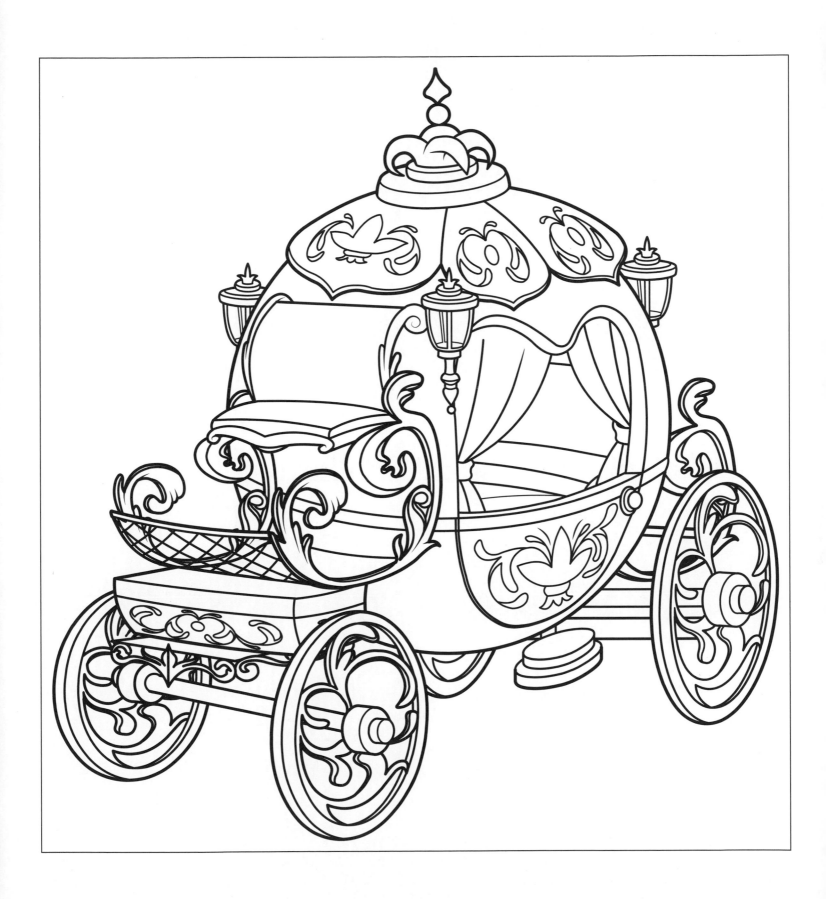

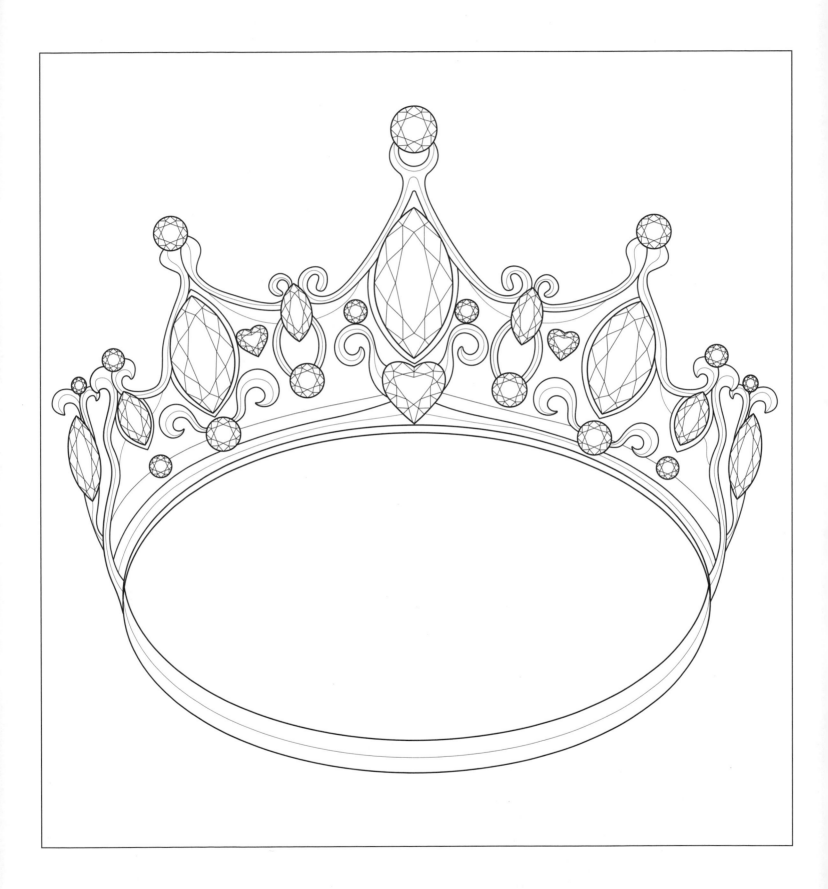

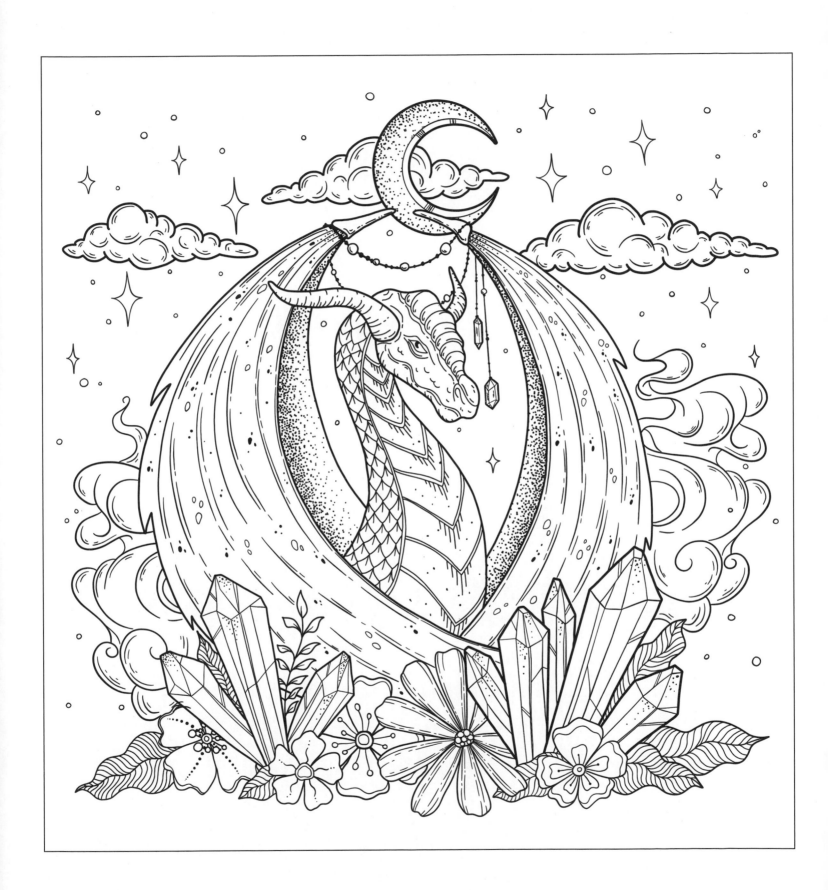

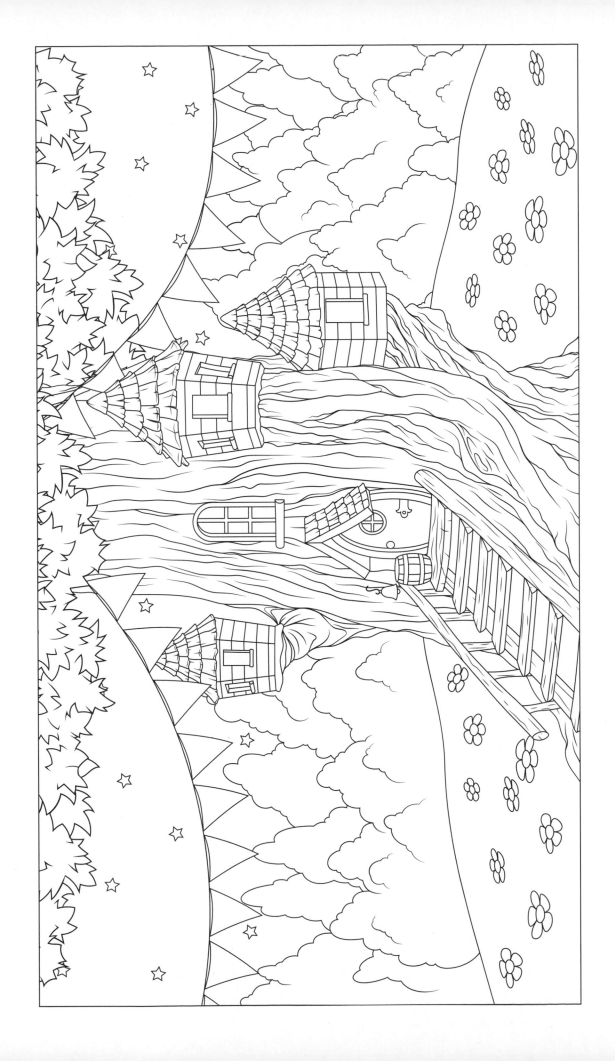

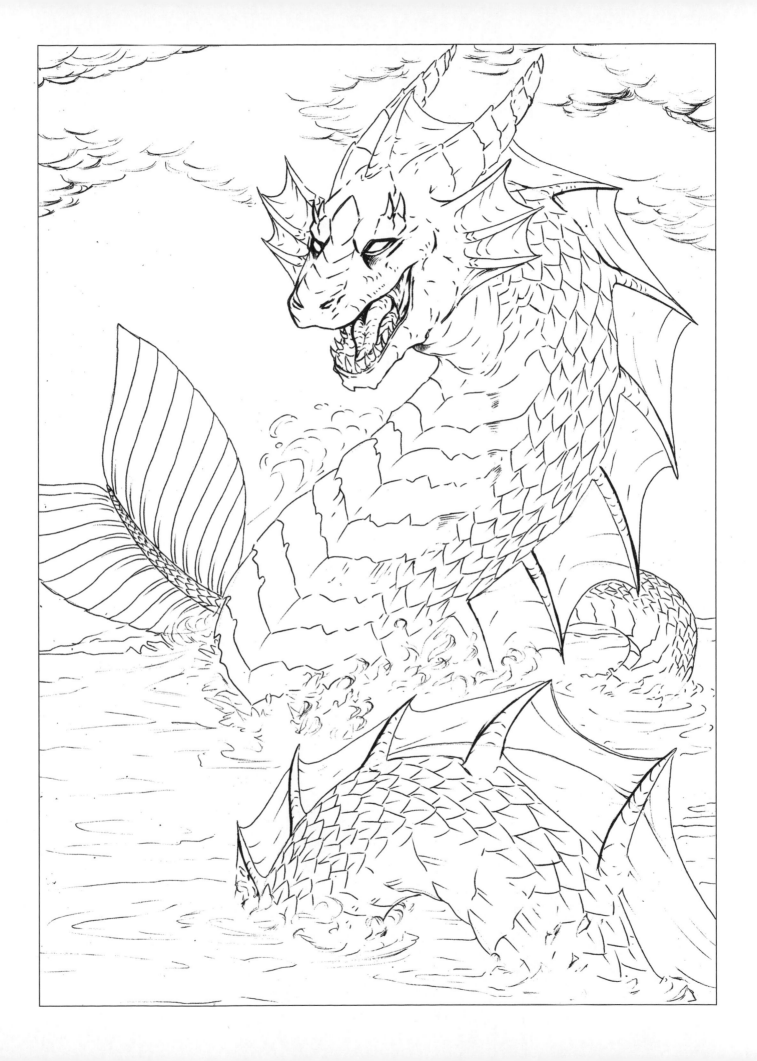

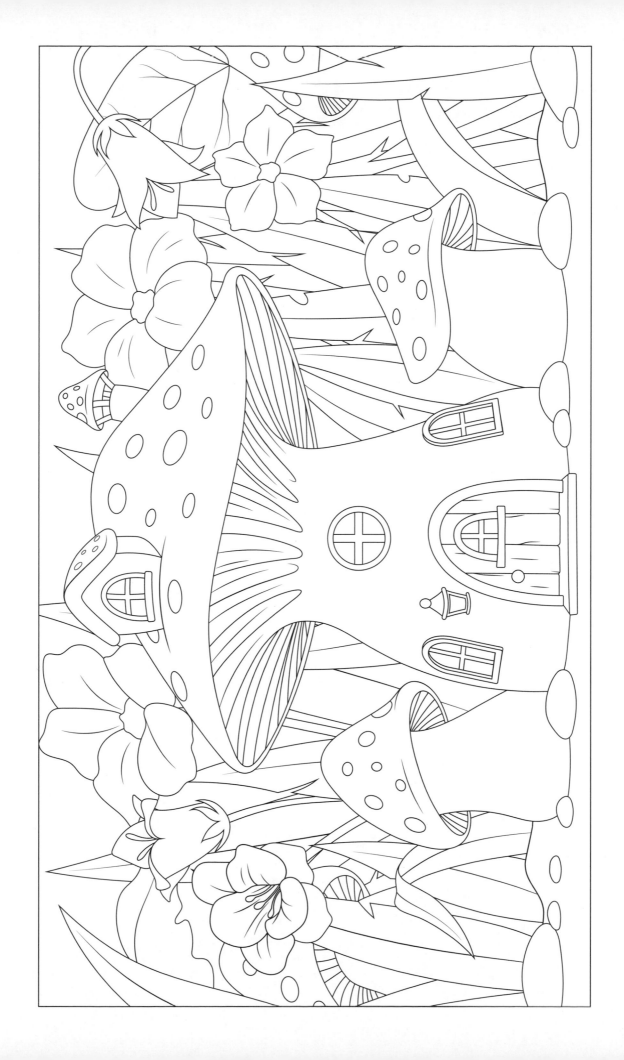

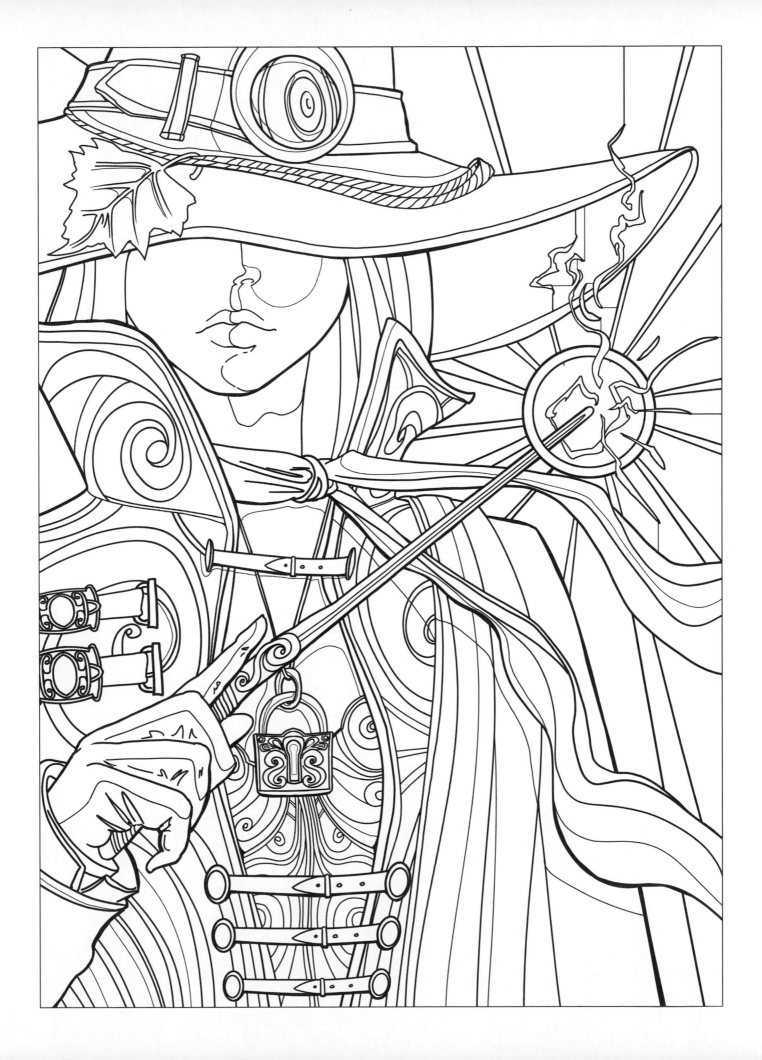

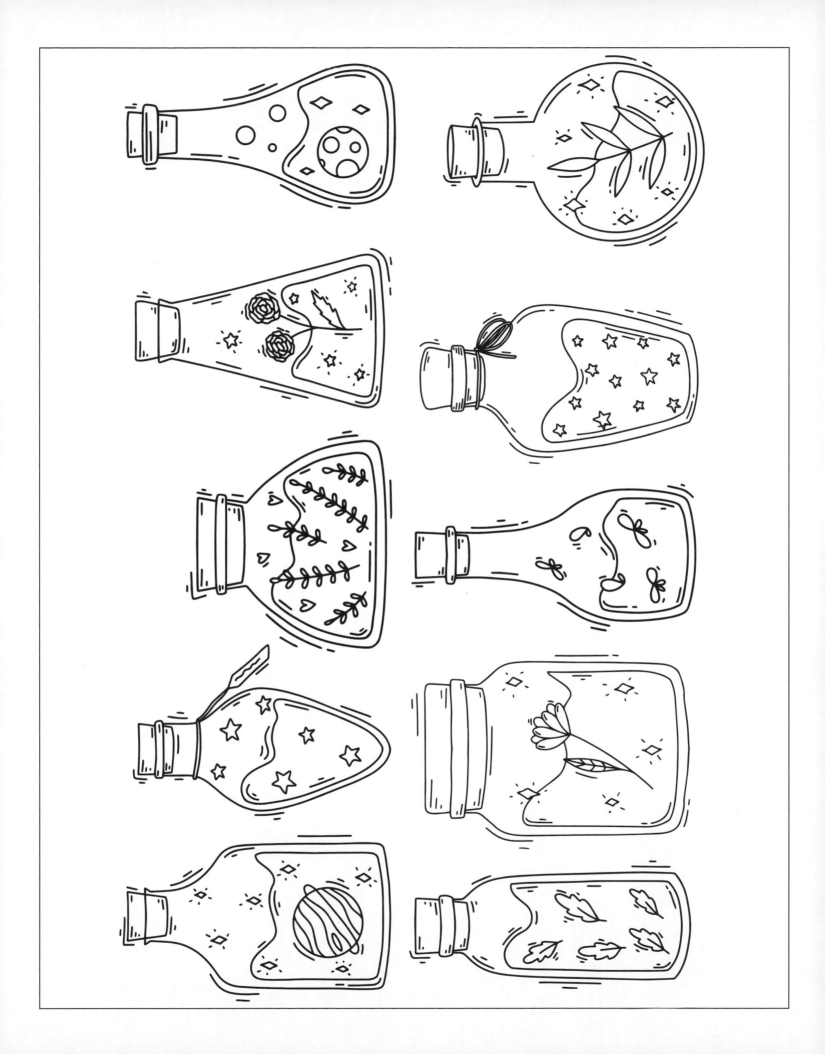

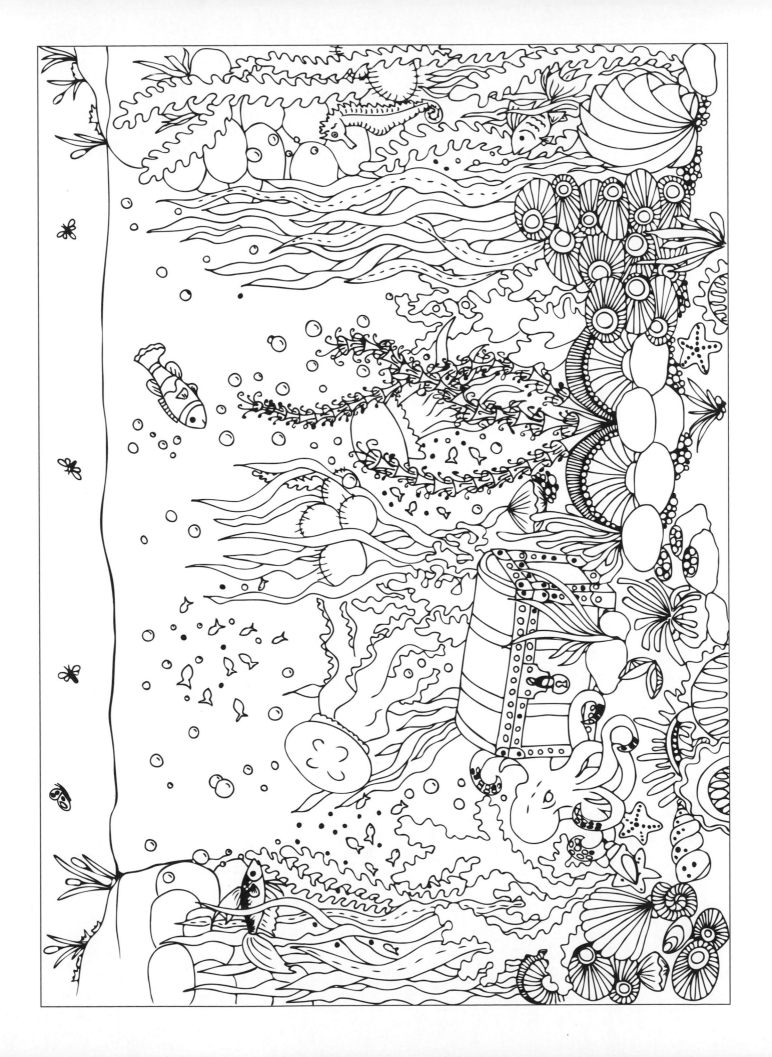

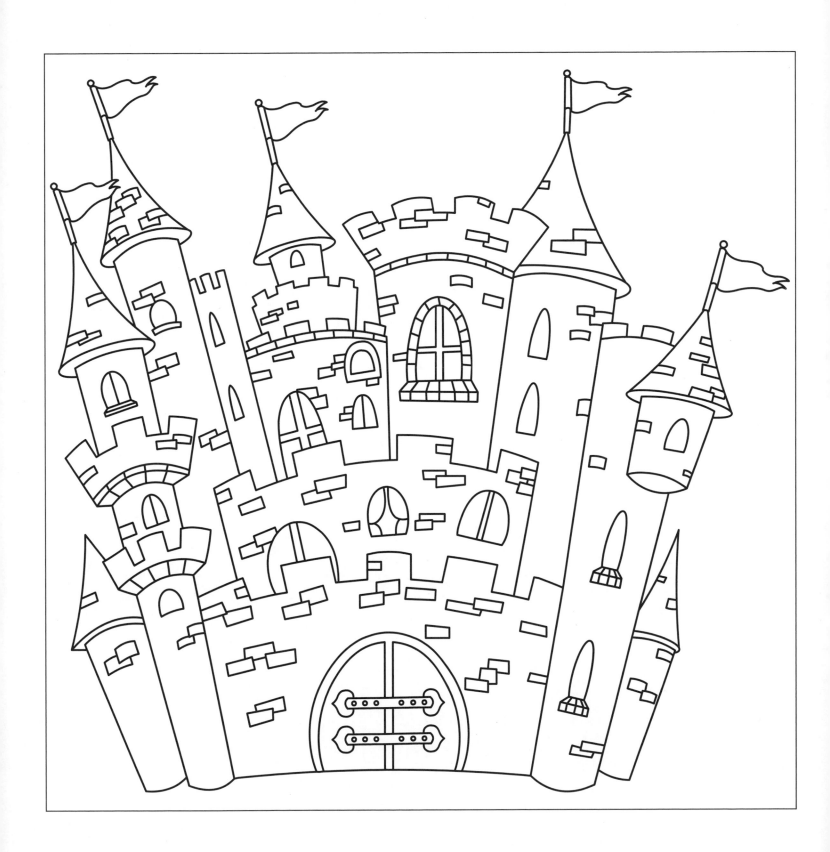

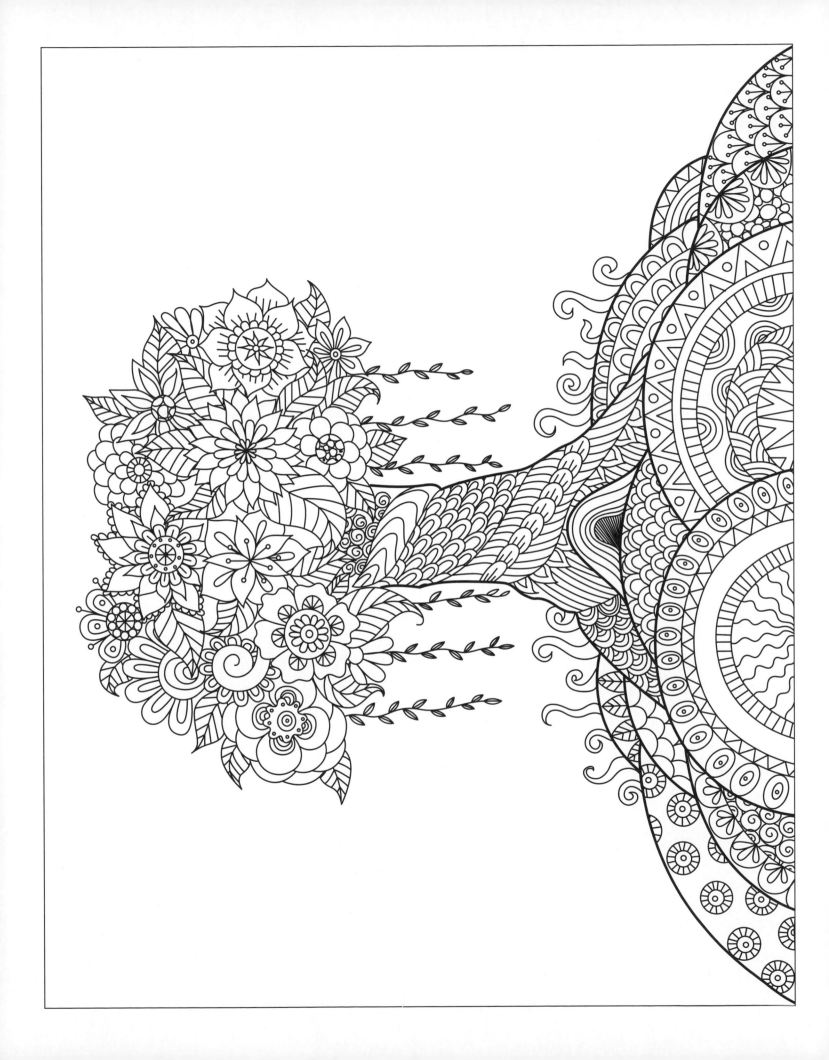

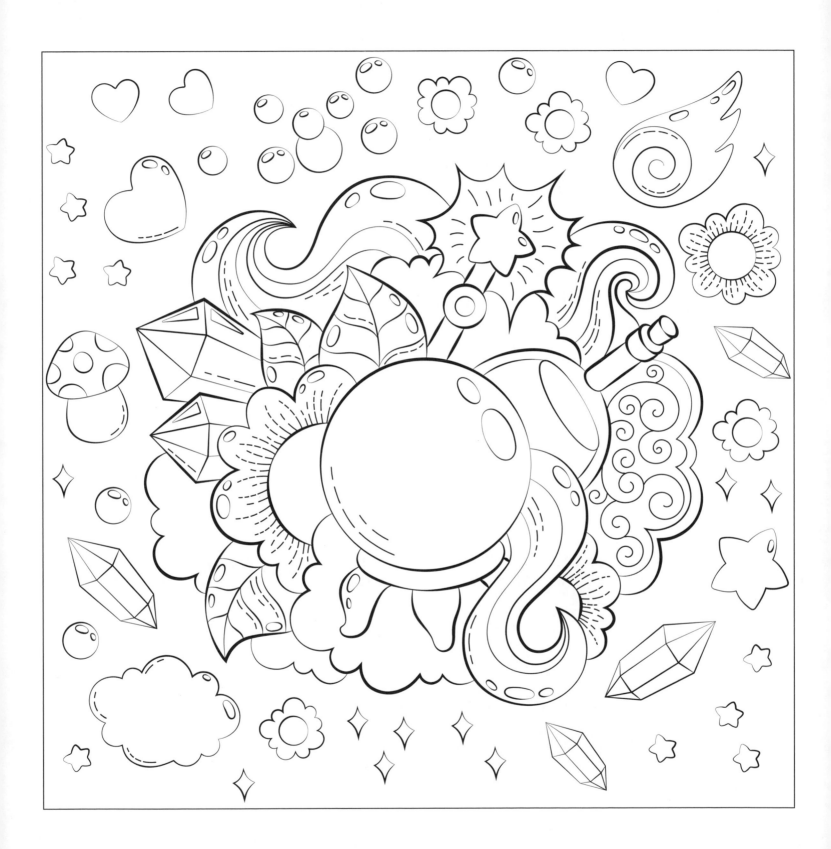

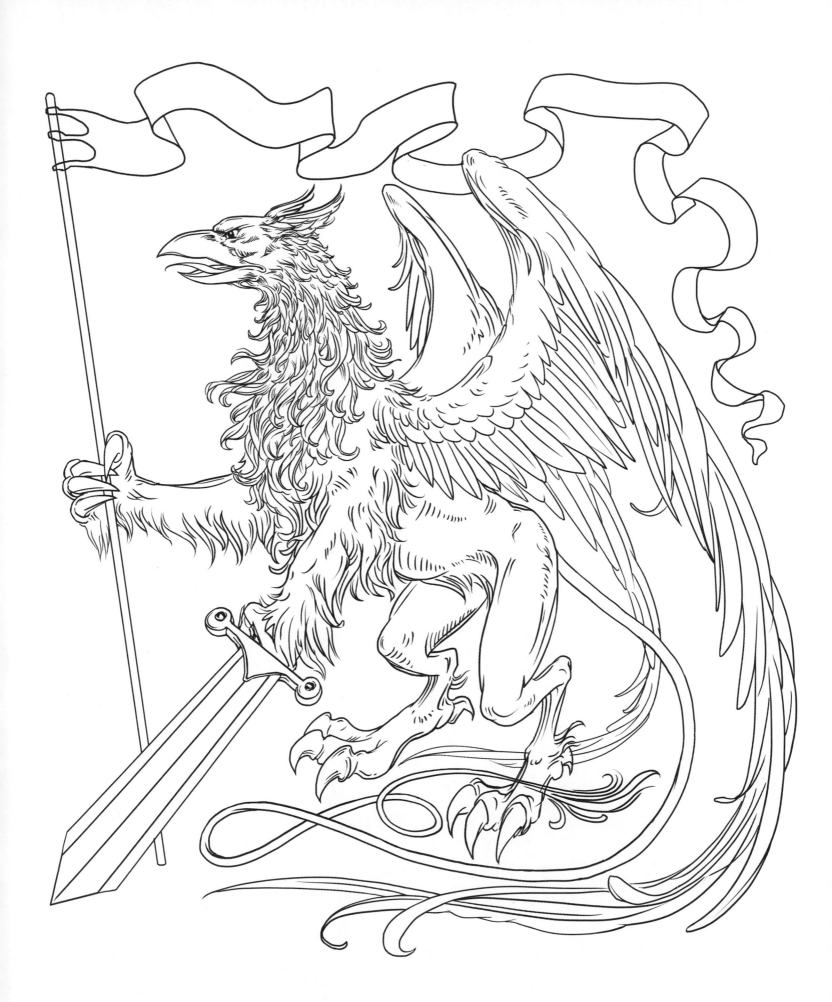

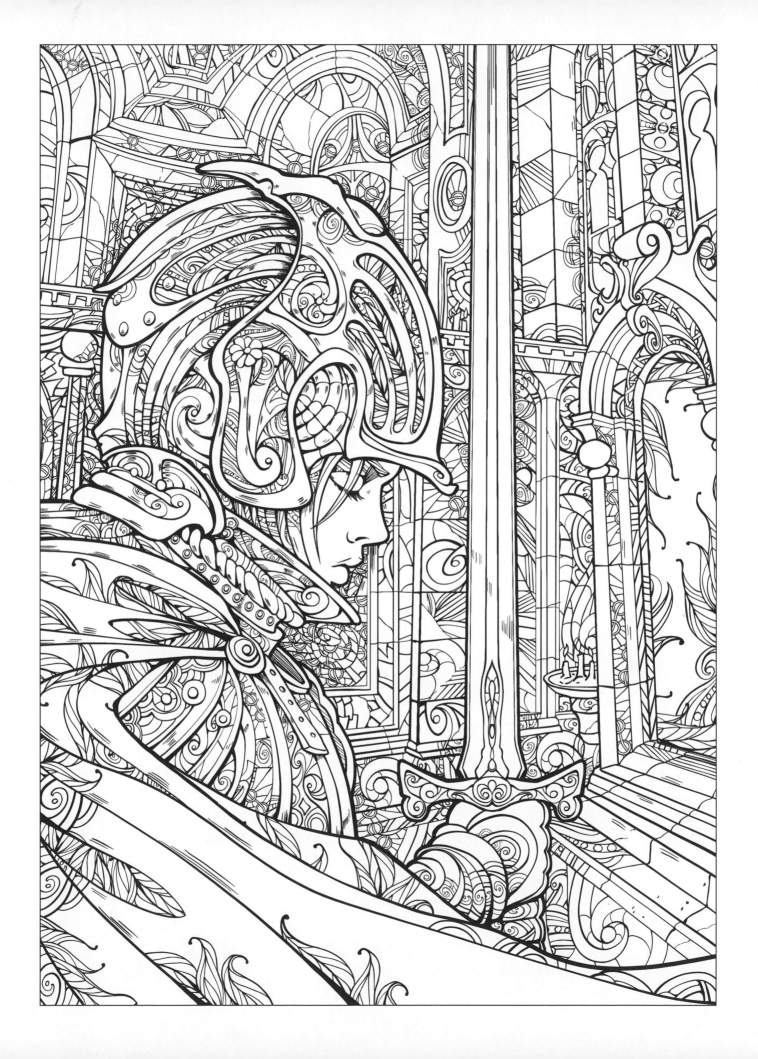

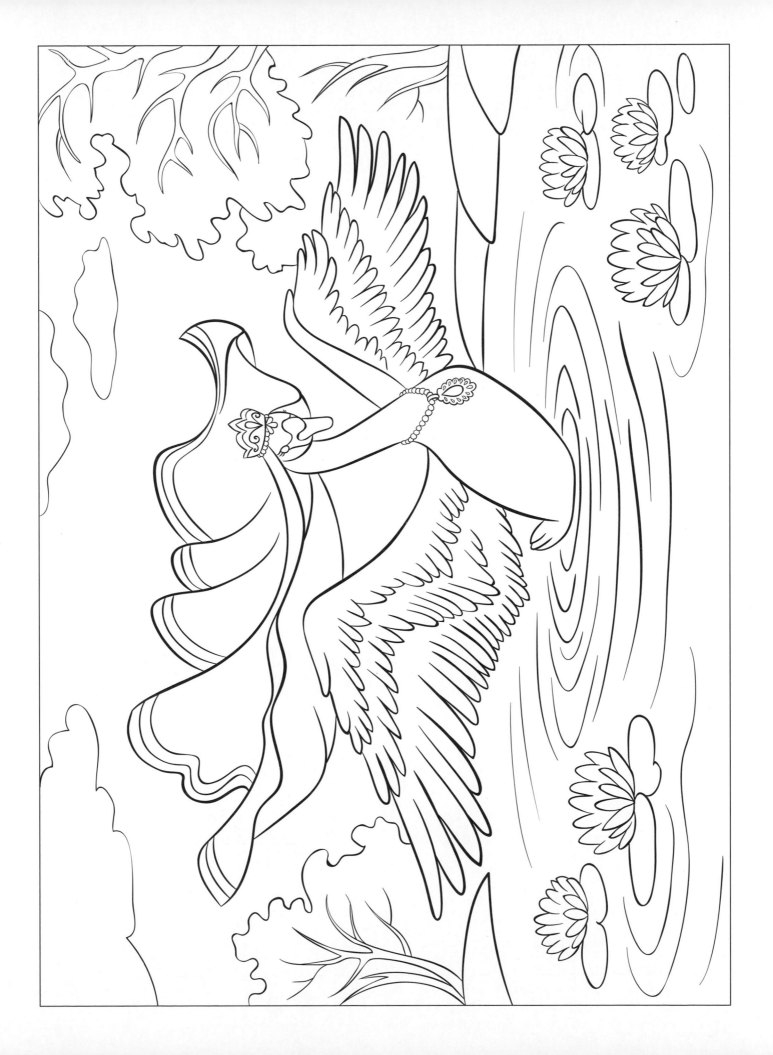

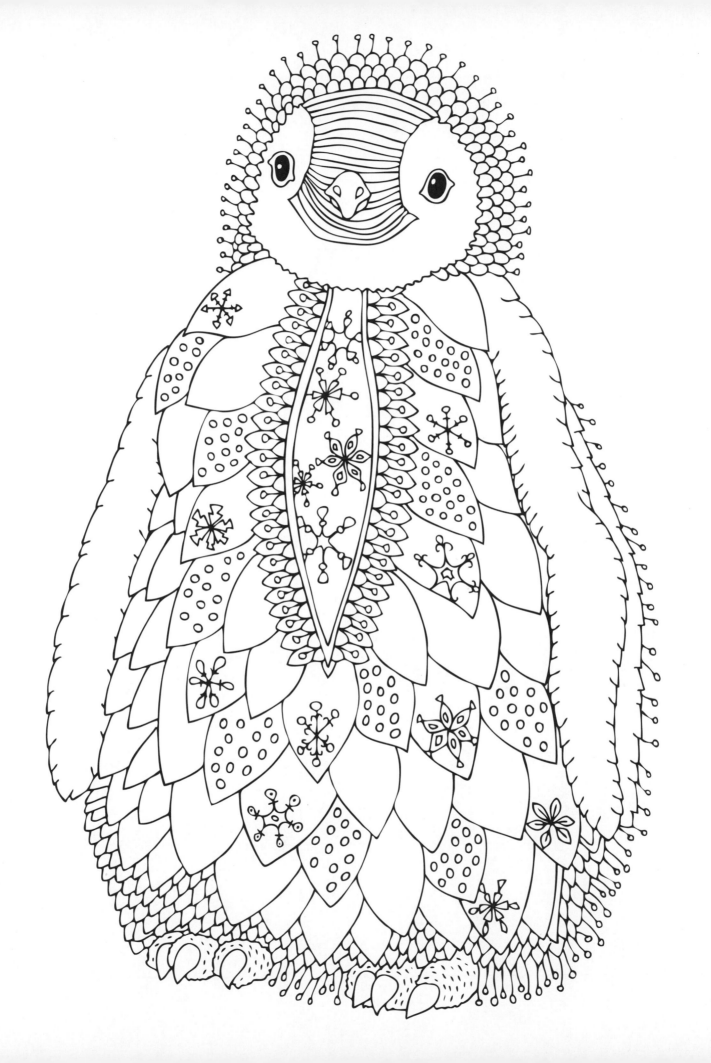

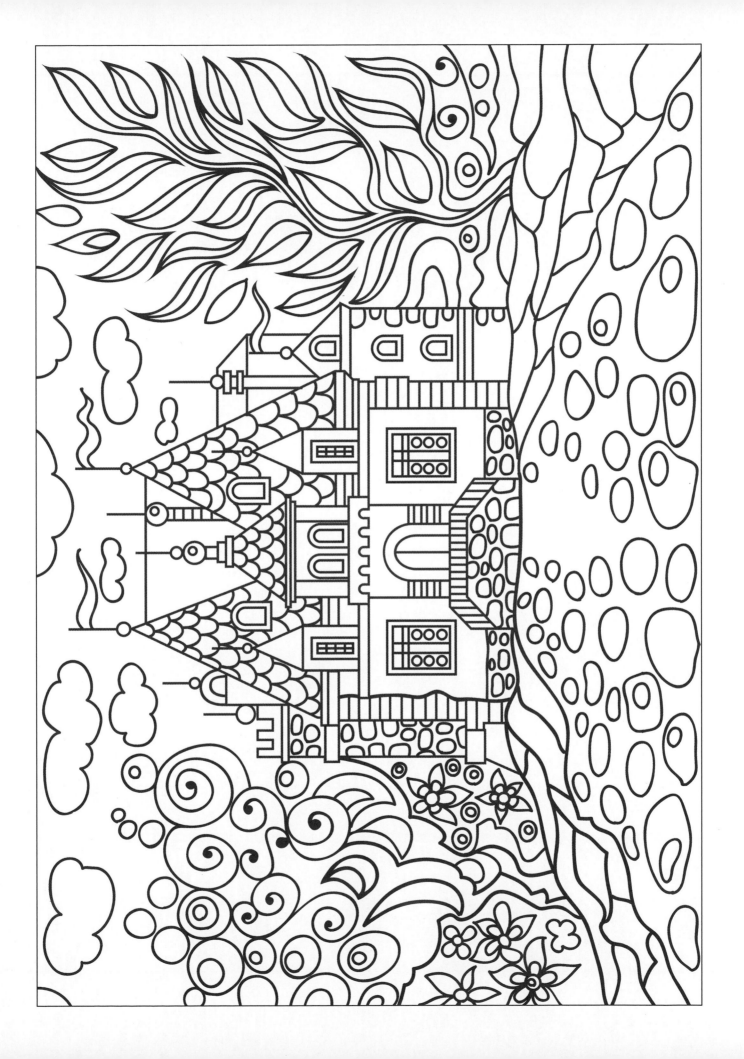

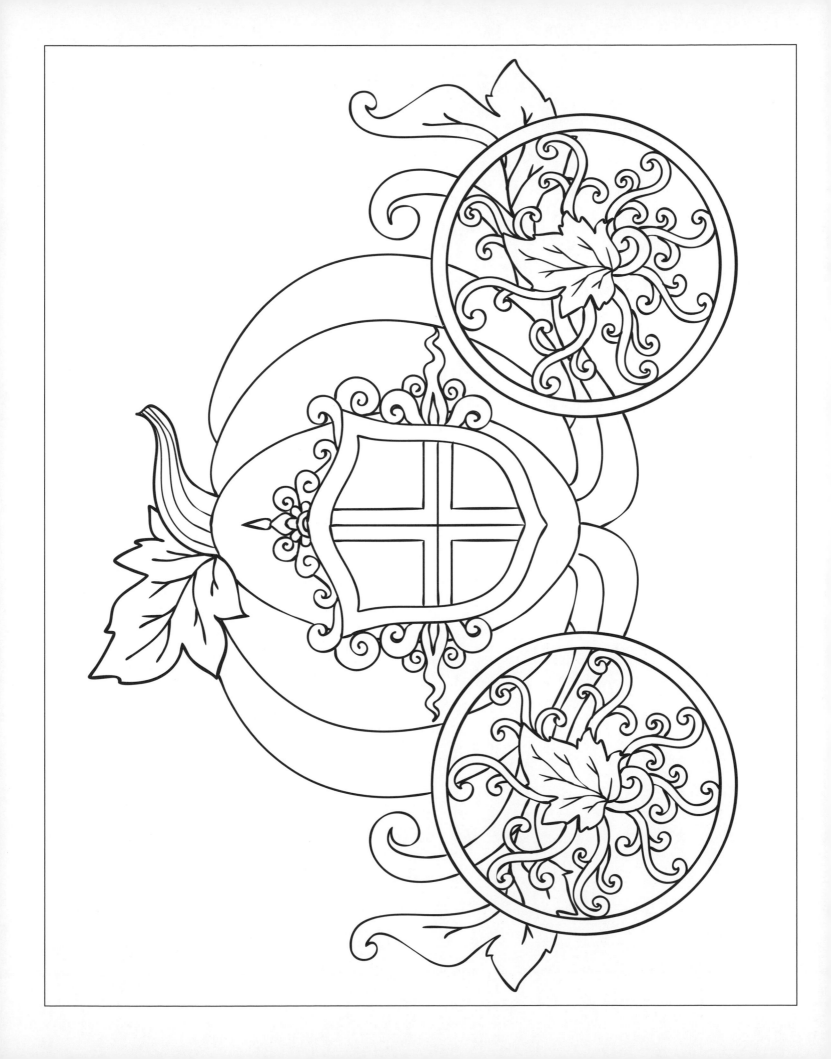

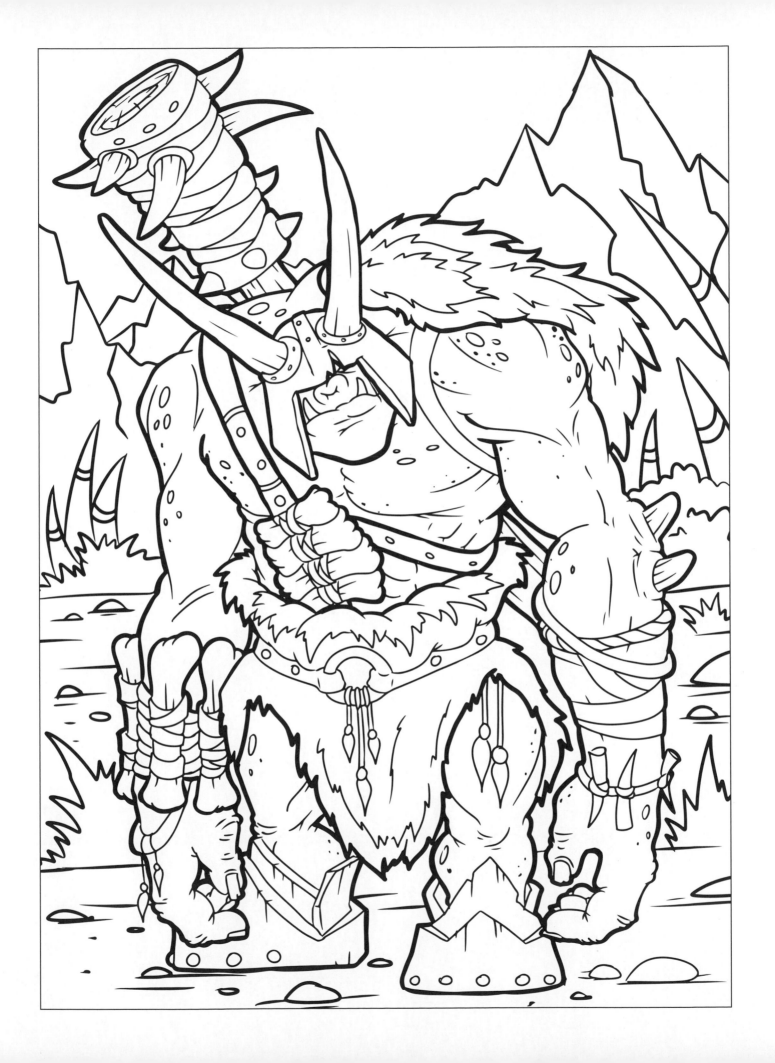

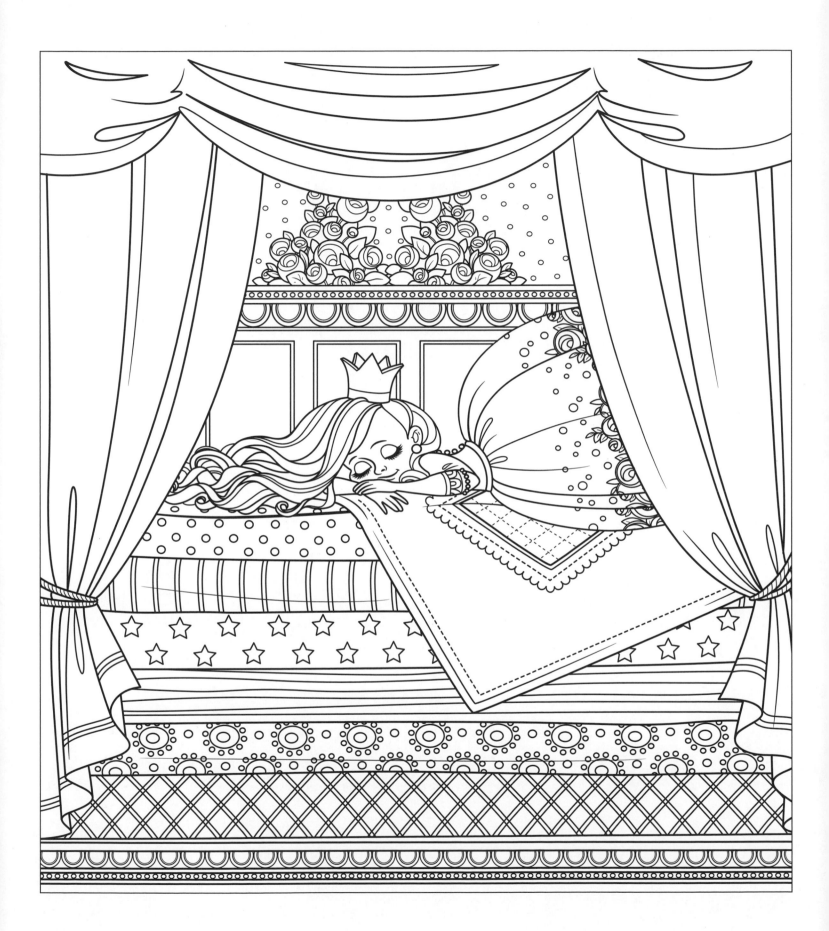

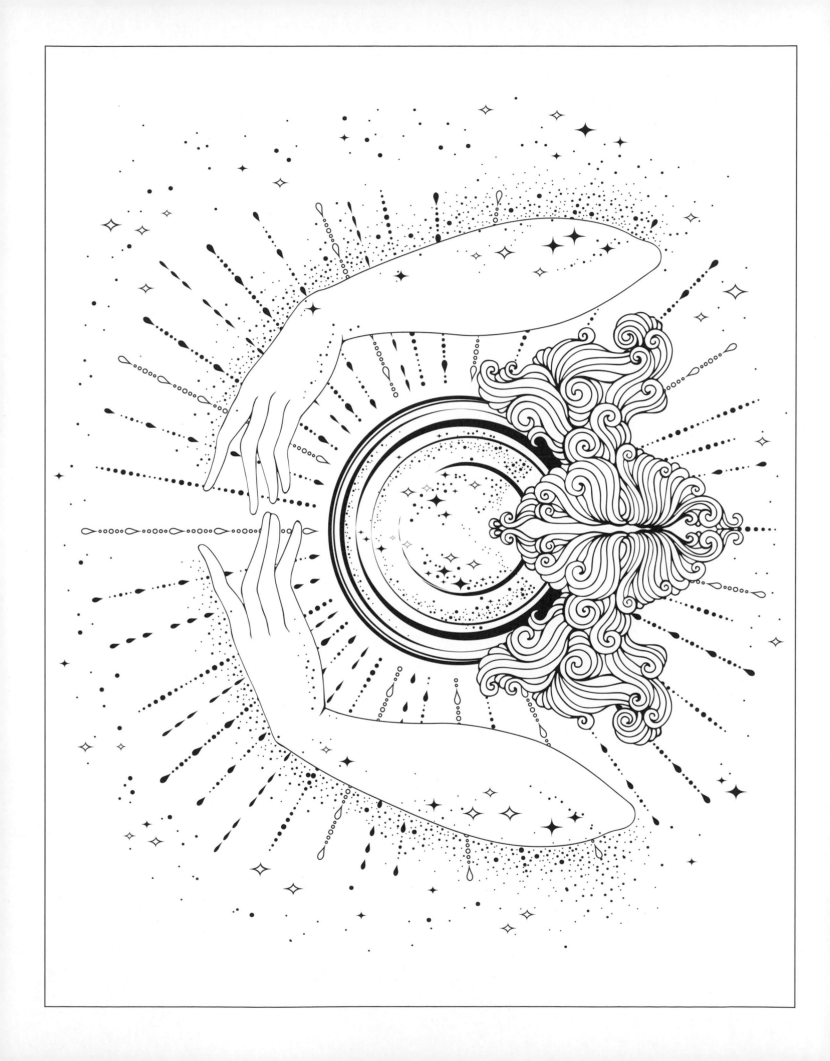

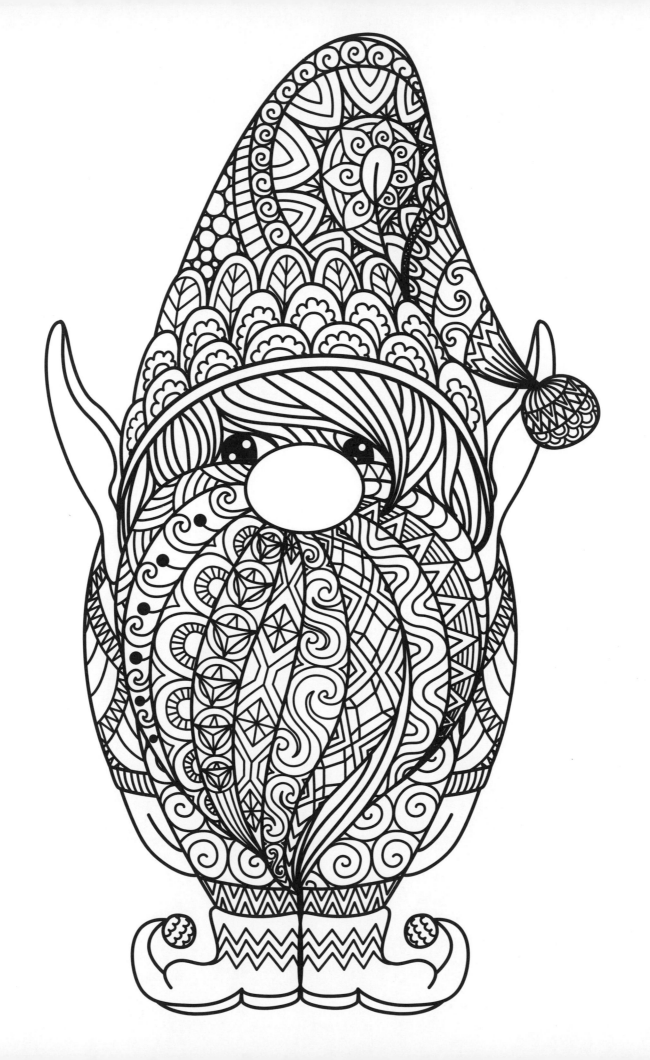

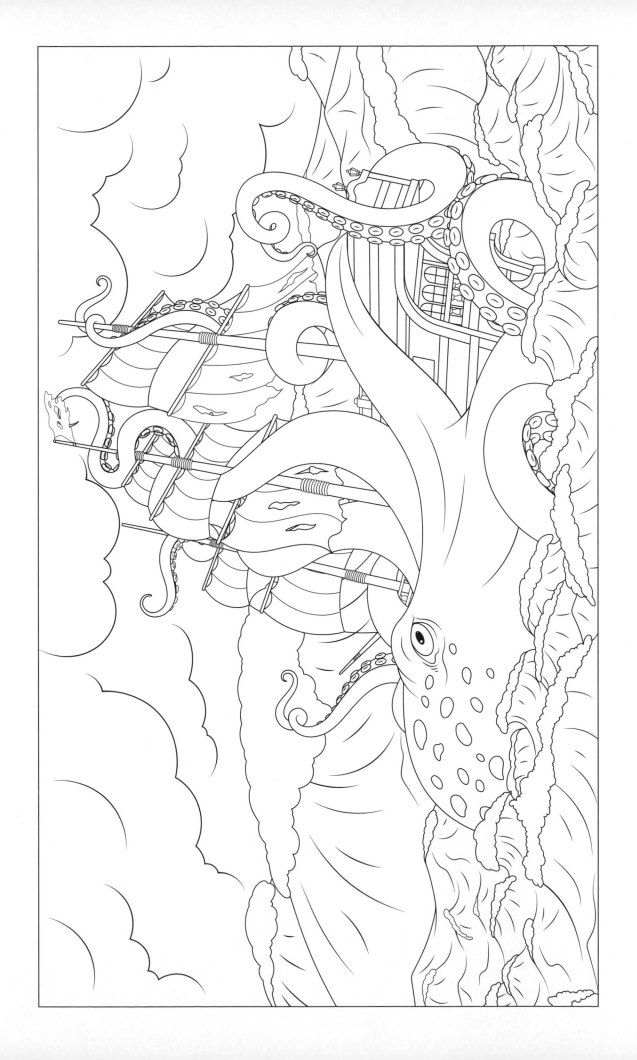

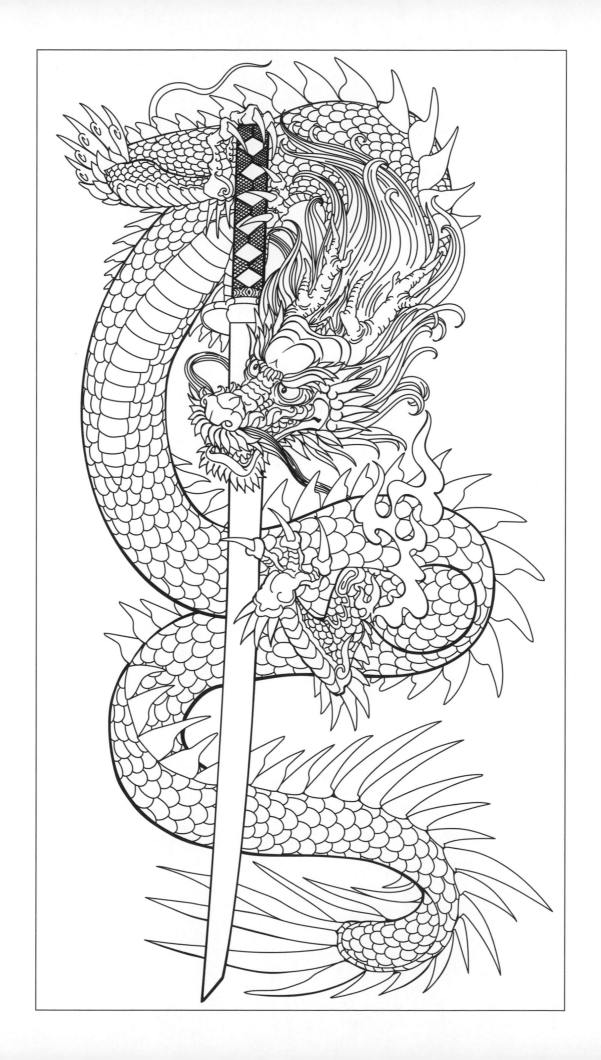

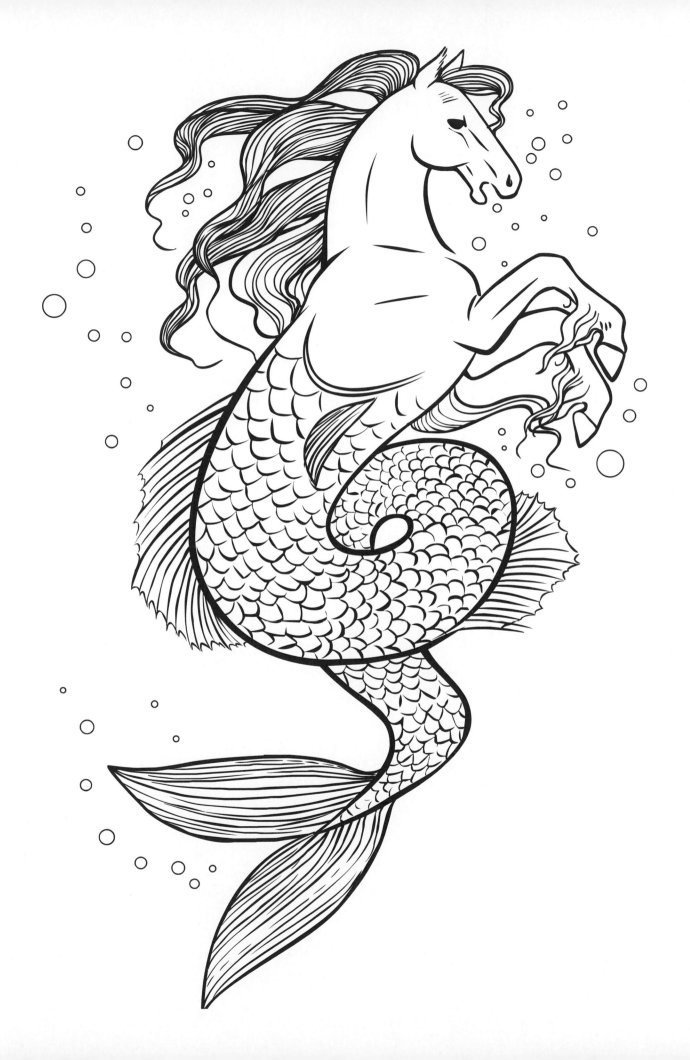

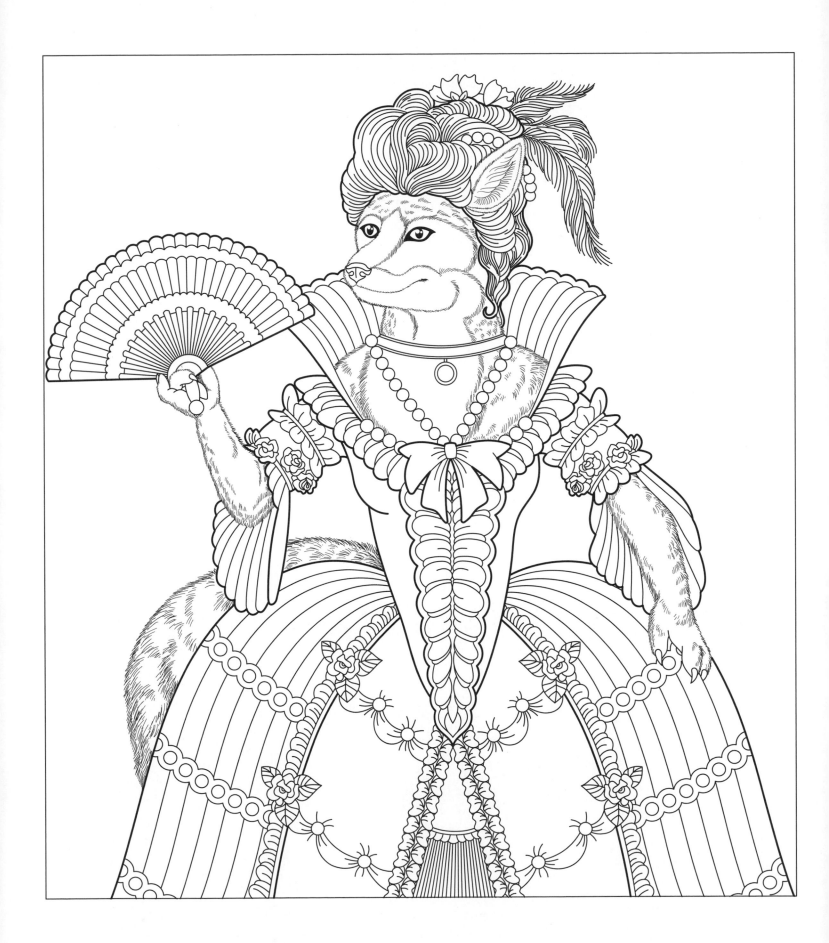

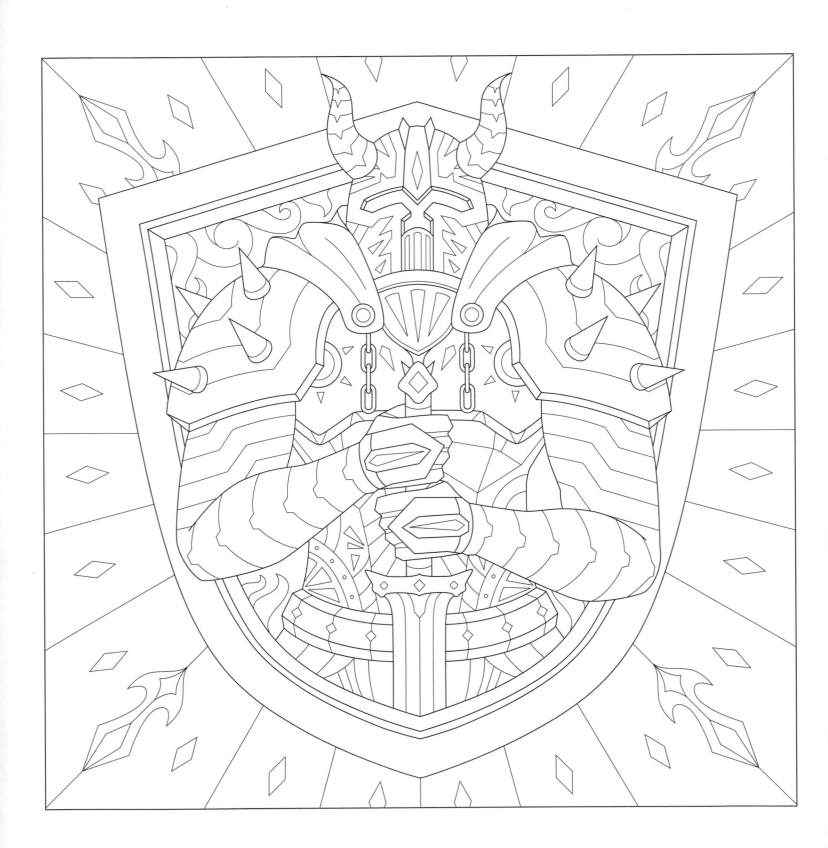

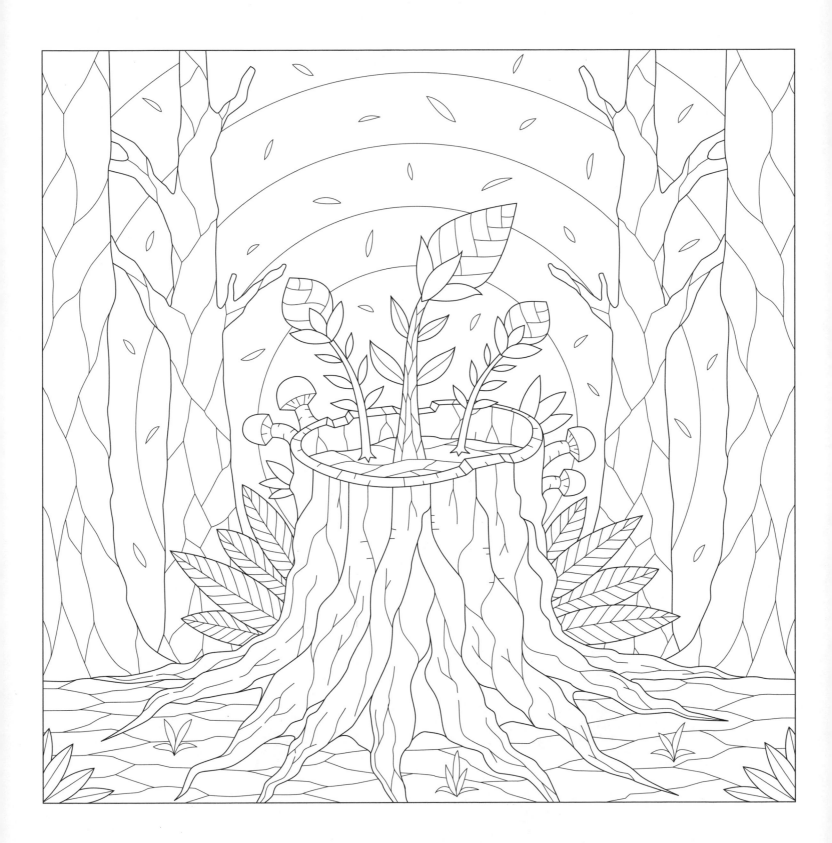

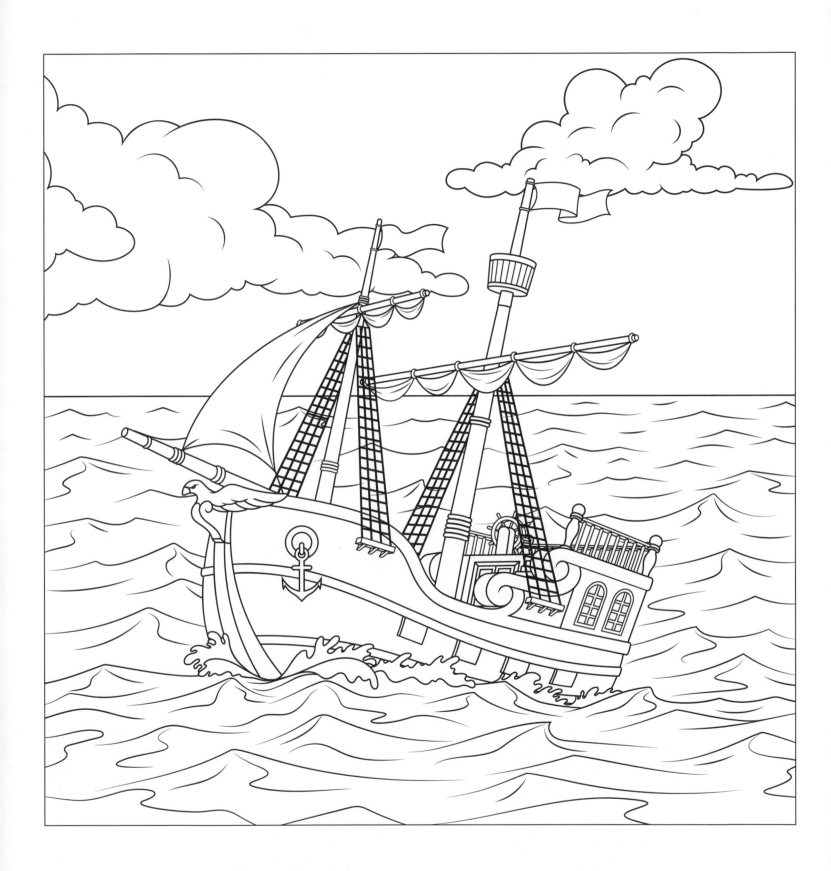

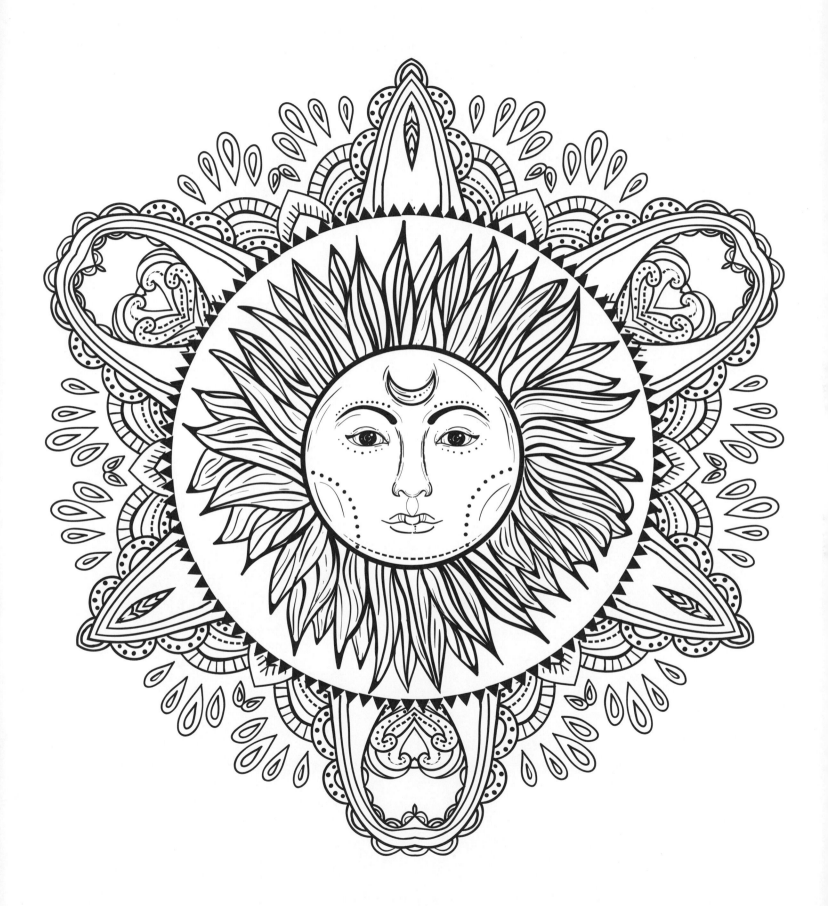

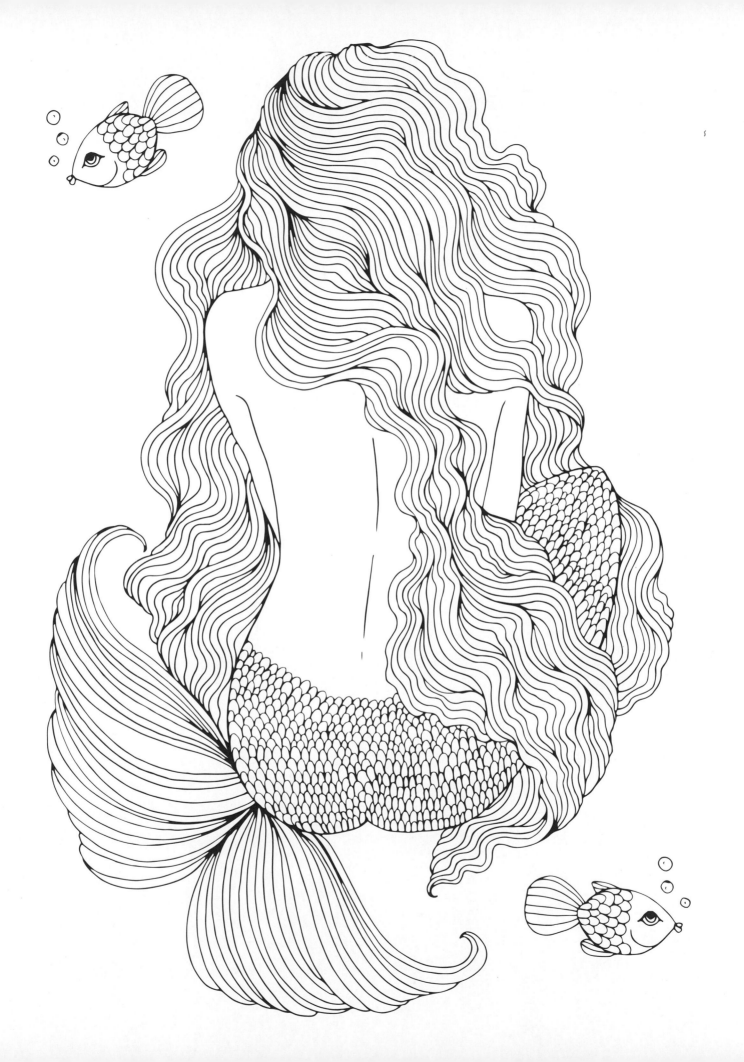

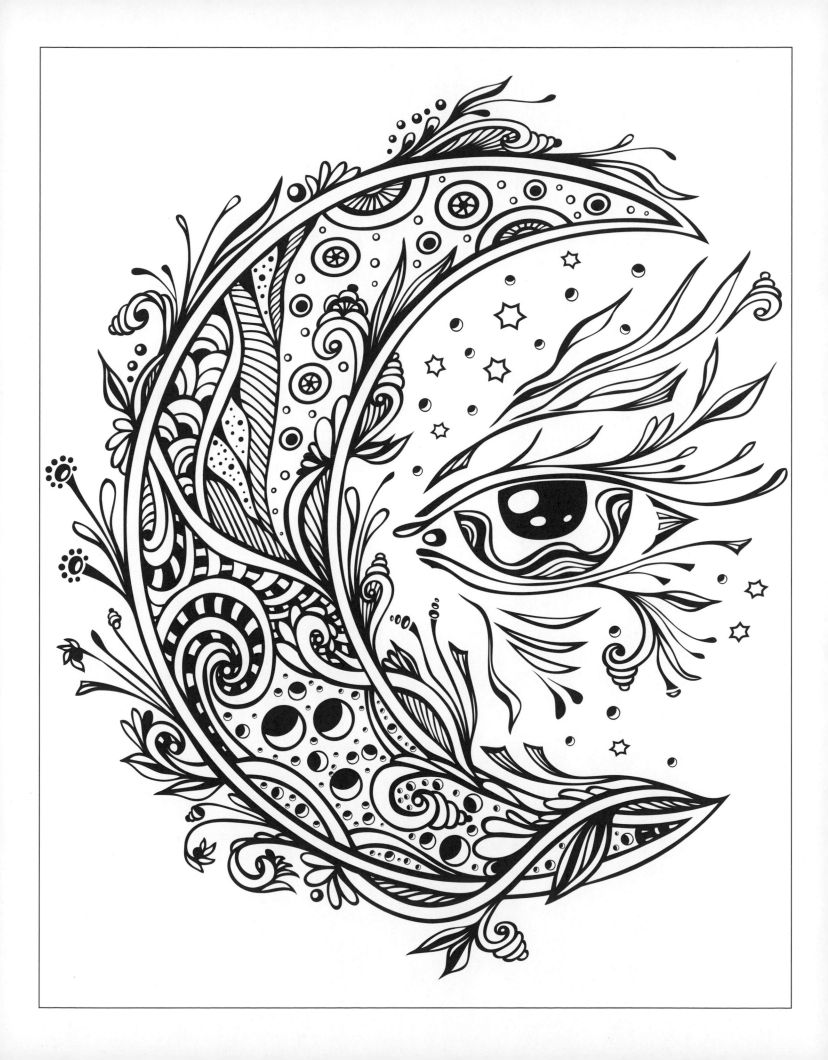

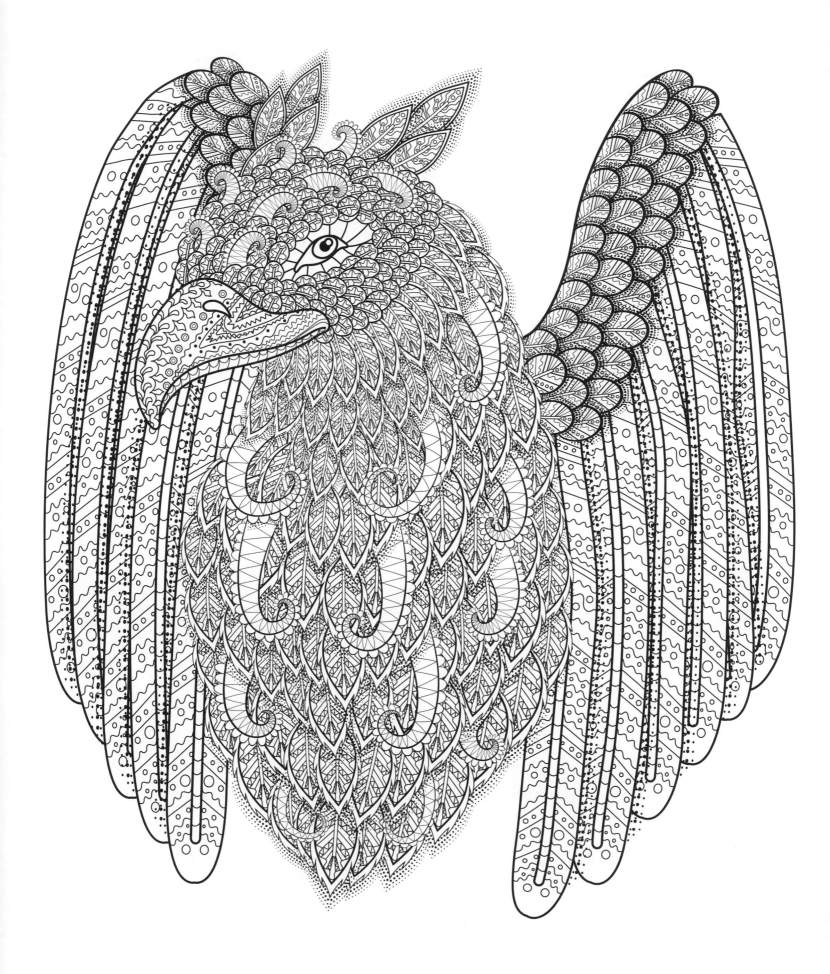

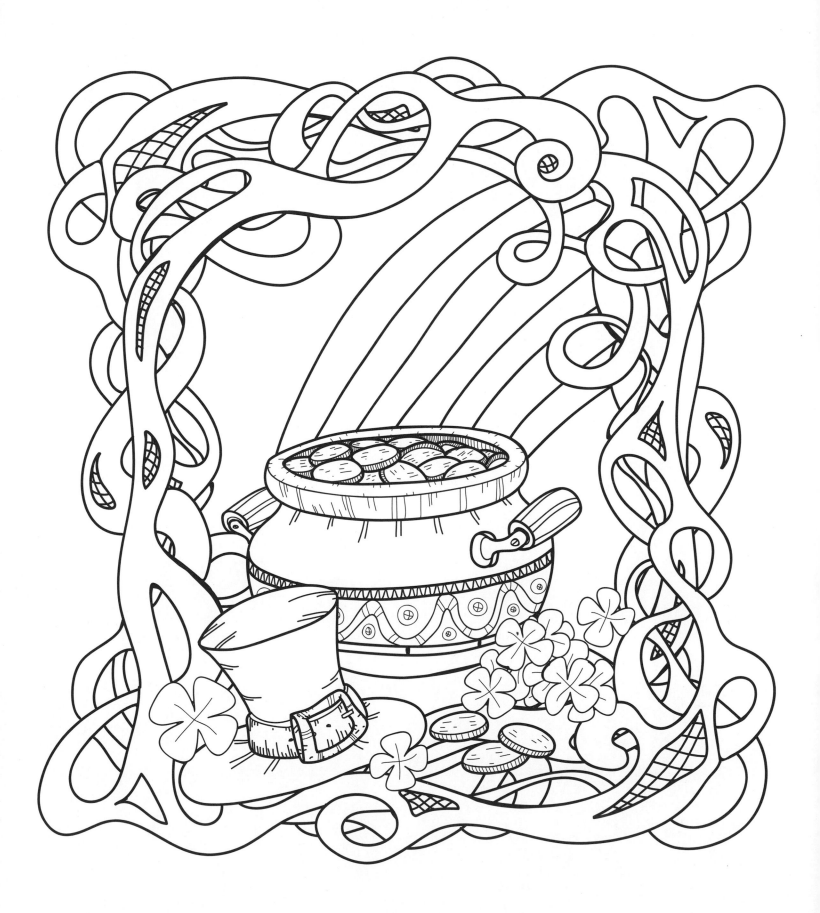

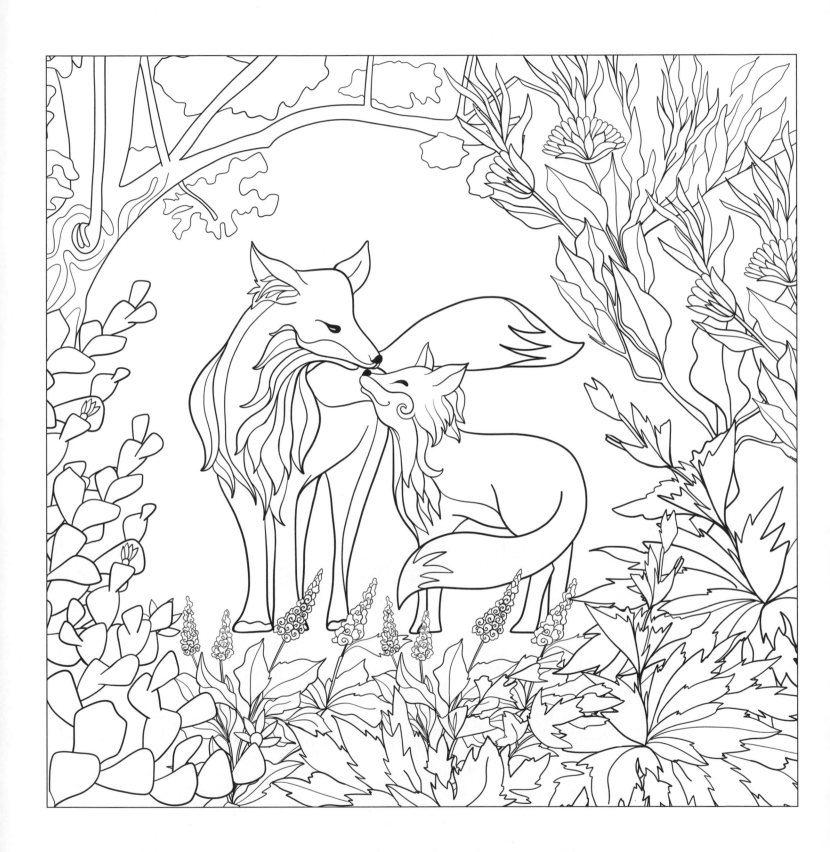

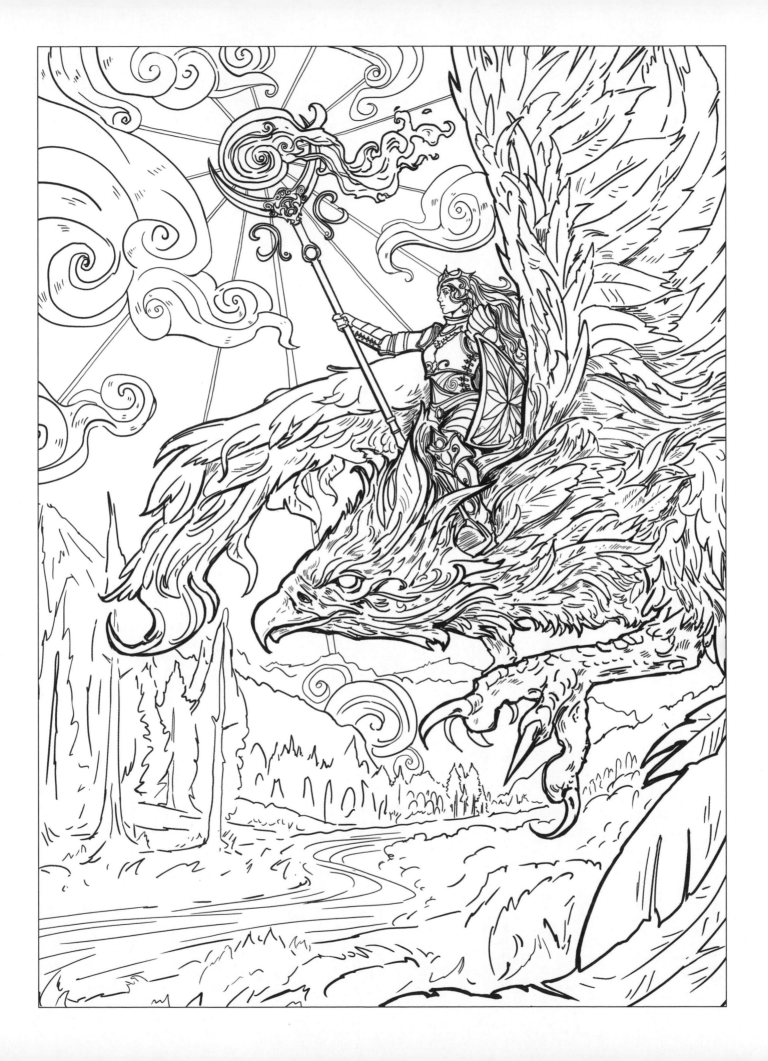

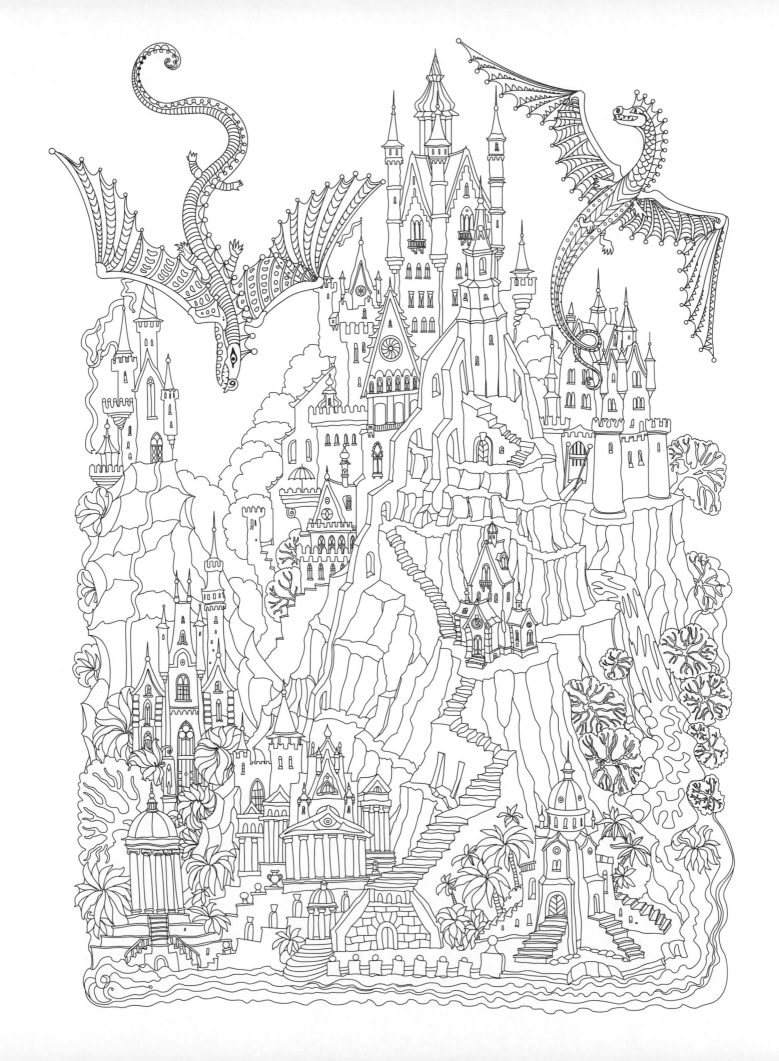

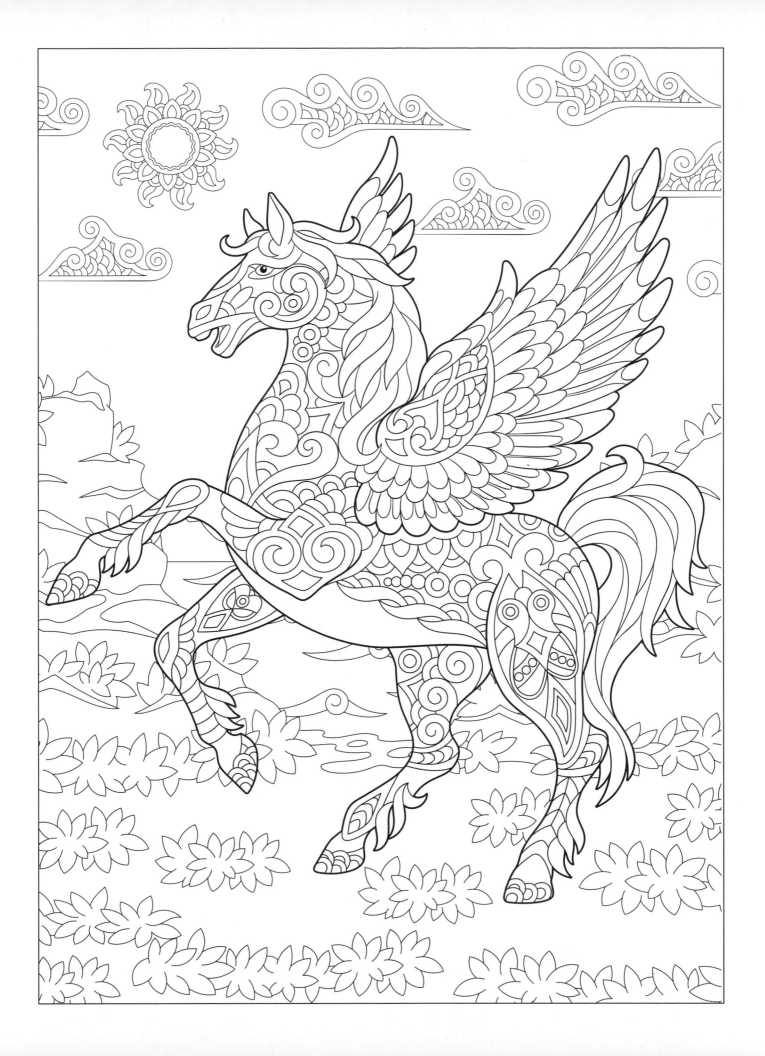

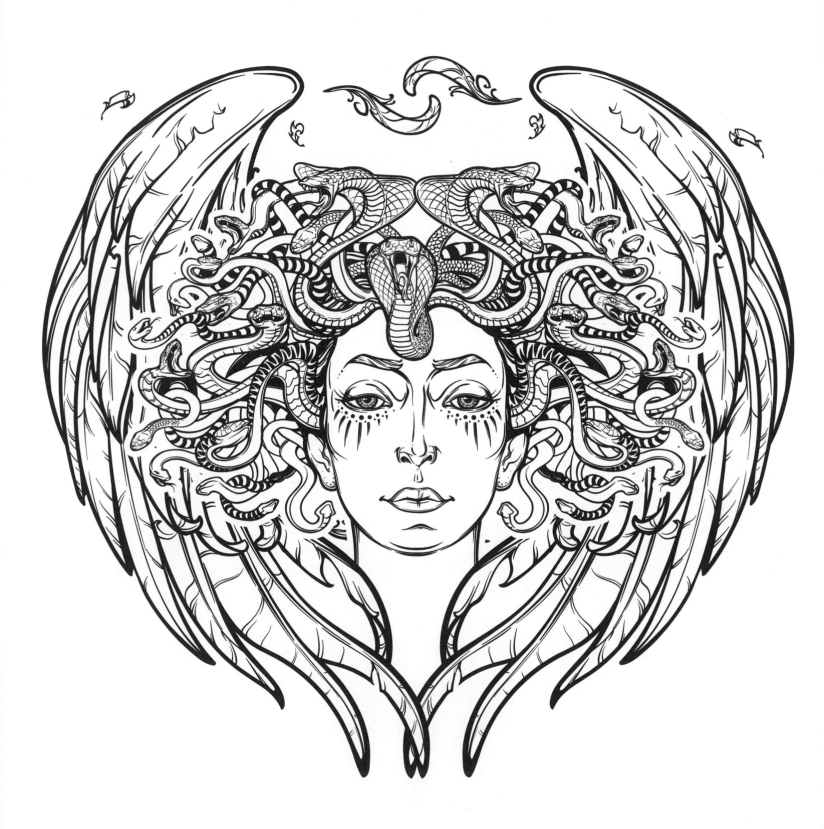

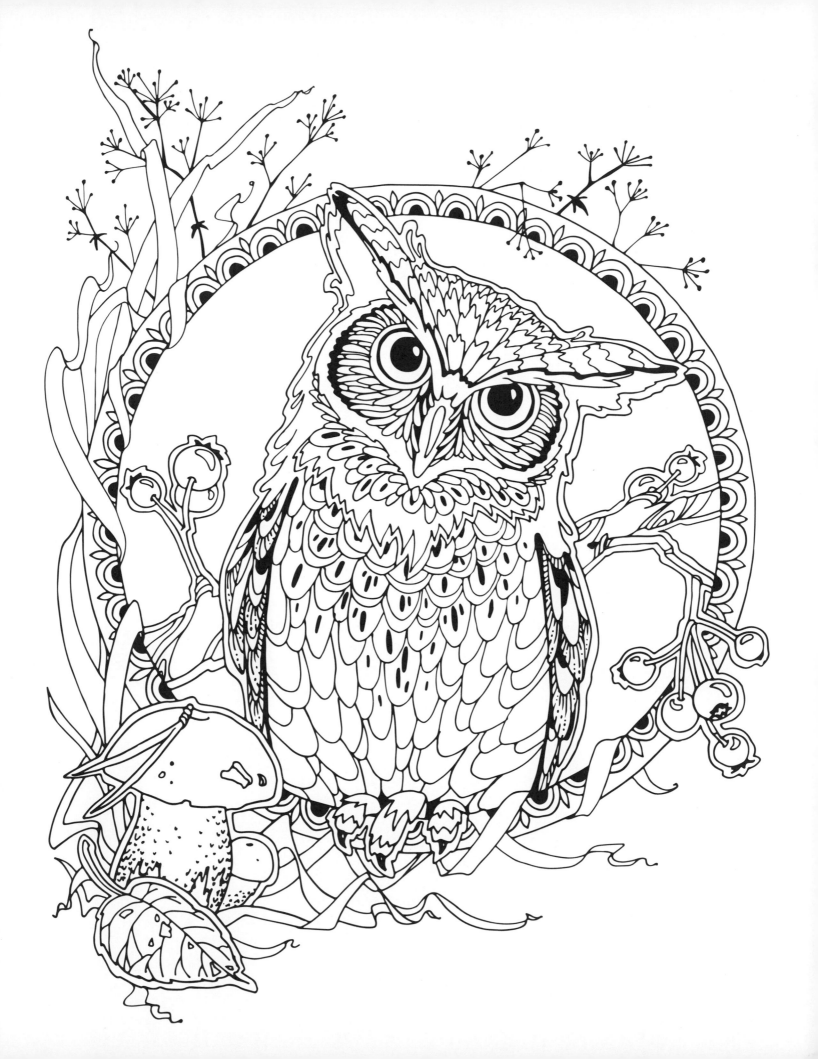

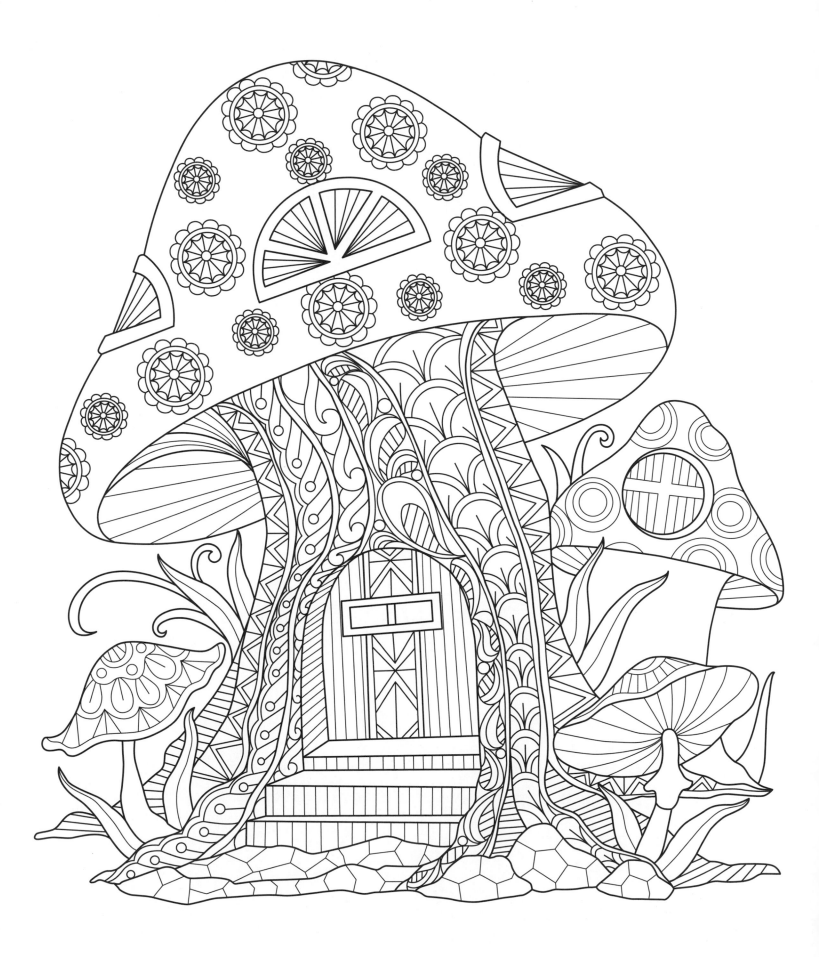

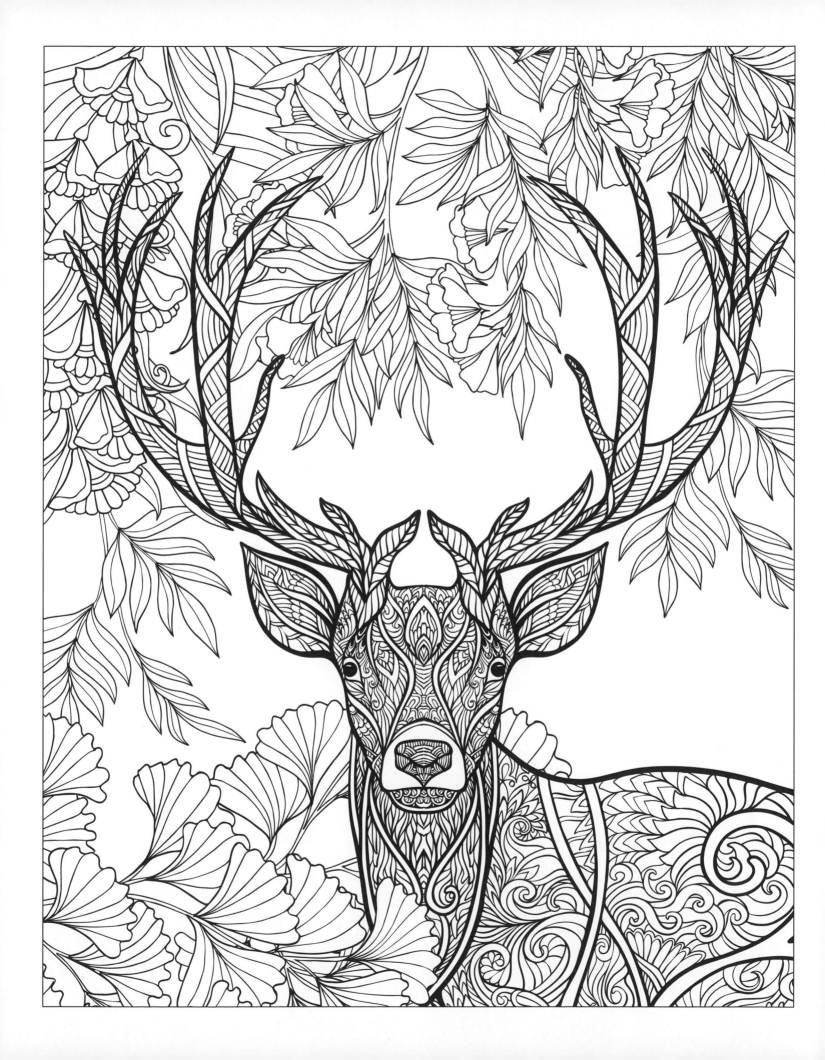

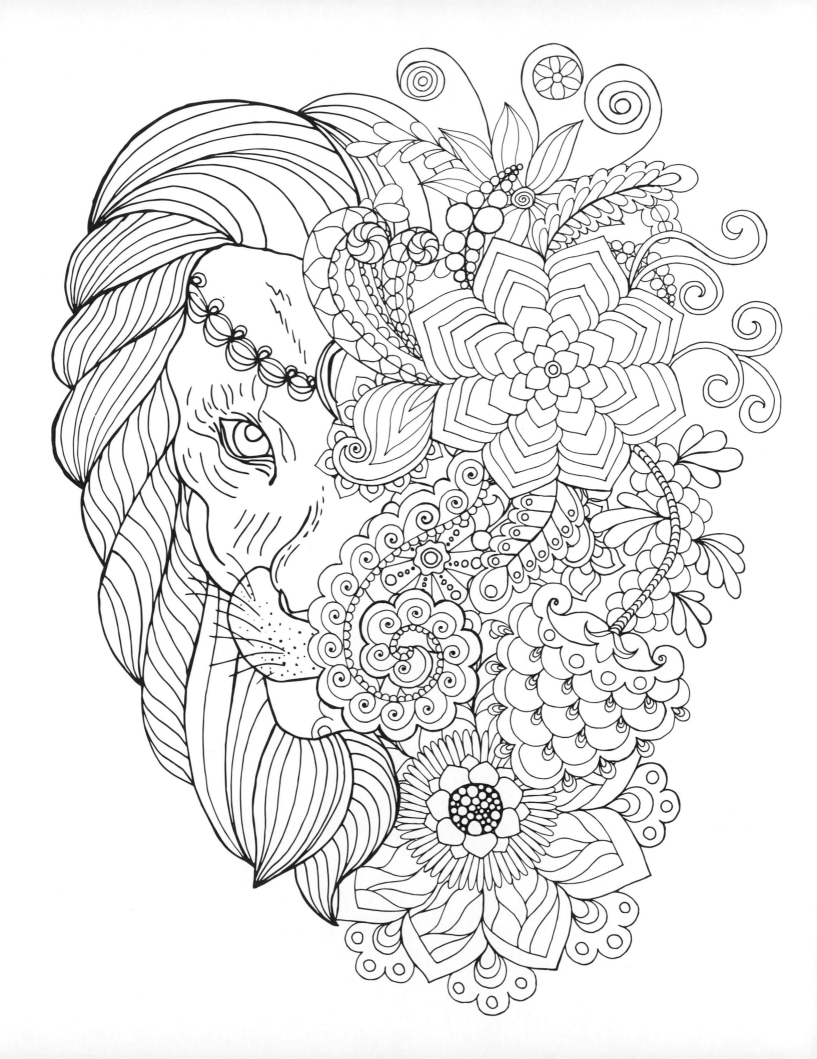

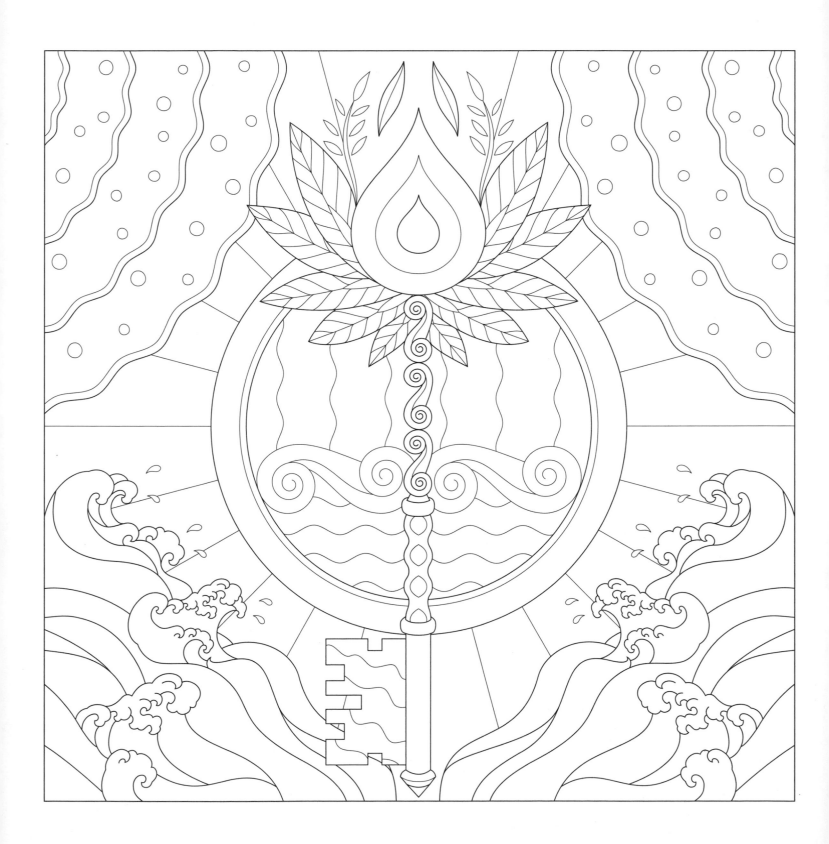

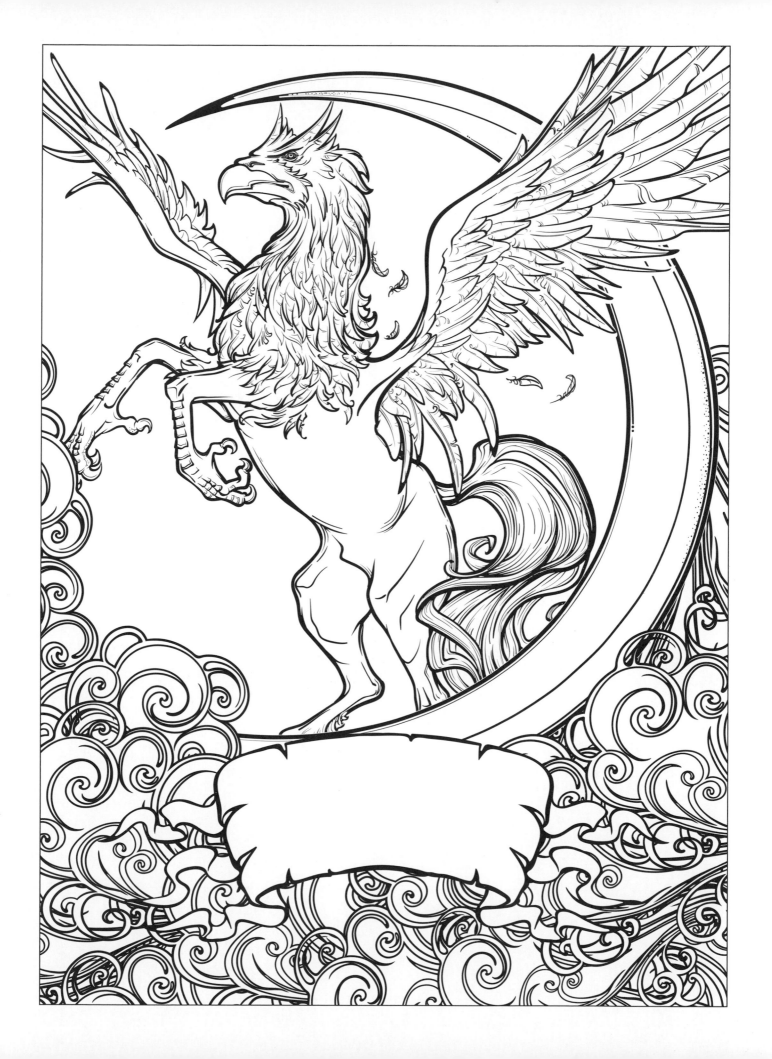